OSPREY COMBAT AIRCRAFT • 70

F-14 TOMCAT UNITS
OF OPERATION
ENDURING FREEDOM

SERIES EDITOR: TONY HOLMES

OSPREY COMBAT AIRCRAFT • 70

F-14 TOMCAT UNITS OF OPERATION *ENDURING FREEDOM*

TONY HOLMES

OSPREY
PUBLISHING

Front cover
VF-102 played a key role in the defence of Tarin Kowt on the morning of 17 November 2001, when Taleban forces from nearby Kandahar threatened to overrun the capital of Uruzgan province. Hours earlier, Pashtun leader, and future Afghan president, Hamid Karzai had sent word to his supporters in Tarin Kowt to start a revolt, and once this was underway, he and his band of fighters moved in. Eleven members of SOF A-Team 574 had also accompanied Karzai into the town.

By dawn on the 17th, an armoured convoy of Taleban tanks, APCs and trucks was only a matter of miles from Tarin Kowt, so SOF combat controllers urgently called in air strikes. The first aircraft to respond were Hornets and Tomcats from CVW-1's VMFA-251 and VF-102, respectively. Flying the lead F-14B (BuNo 163225) in the 'Diamondbacks'' section was the unit's maintenance officer and his RIO. Over the next two hours, they provided more than 30 FAC(A) controls for Hornets and Tomcats dropping precision-guided munitions and Mk 83 airburst bombs (the latter exclusively from F-14Bs).

Despite the employment of overwhelming air power, the Taleban force continued to home in on Tarin Kowt. During a lull in the action, when more CVW-1 strike aircraft were still minutes away from the target, the enemy attempted to take advantage of this situation by pressing on towards their objective in an assortment of vehicles, including a tank. Still overhead Tarin Kowt, the crew of BuNo 163225, and their wingman, had by now used all their LGBs, and only had their 20 mm cannon left to repel this attack.

'The cannon was our weapon of last resort, as we had run out of ordnance and there was no one available to relieve us on station', the maintenance officer explained. 'We didn't want to strafe, but we had no choice, as the nearest jet with bombs was ten minutes away.

'We had spoken about strafing within the squadron during our work-ups, and agreed that the gun would only be used as a weapon of last resort in a danger close situation. With the tank clearly on the move, we went for a classical forward quarter attack. My wingman strafed first, and his gun jammed

after he had fired just a single burst. We then came in from the same direction and made two passes, and although I am uncertain as to whether we hit the tank or not, it stopped and at least one crewman got out. A third pass was made on a truck that was also on the move, and it too was stopped in its tracks.'

Thanks to the naval aviators' persistence overhead the target area, Tarin Kowt was never recaptured by the Taleban. For their efforts on this day, VF-102's maintenance officer and his RIO were each awarded the Distinguished Flying Cross (*Cover artwork by Mark Postlethwaite*)

First published in Great Britain in 2008 by Osprey Publishing
Midland House, West Way, Botley, Oxford, OX2 0PH
443 Park Avenue South, New York, NY, 10016, USA
E-mail; info@ospreypublishing.com

© 2008 Osprey Publishing Limited

ISBN 13: 978 1 84603 205 9

Written & Edited by Tony Holmes
Page design by Tony Truscott
Cover Artwork by Mark Postlethwaite
Aircraft Profiles by Jim Laurier
Index by Alan Thatcher
Printed in China

08 09 10 11 12   10 9 8 7 6 5 4 3 2 1

For a catalogue of all books published by Osprey please contact:
NORTH AMERICA
Osprey Direct, c/o Random House Distribution Center, 400 Hahn Road, Westminster, MD 21157. E-mail: info@ospreydirect.com

ALL OTHER REGIONS
Osprey Direct UK, P.O. Box 140 Wellingborough, Northants, NN8 2FA, UK.
E-mail: info@ospreydirect.co.uk
(www.ospreypublishing.com)

EDITOR'S NOTE
To make this best-selling series as authoritative as possible, the Editor would be interested in hearing from any individual who may have relevant photographs, documentation or first-hand experiences relating to the world's elite pilots, and their aircraft, of the various theatres of war. Any material used will be credited to its original source. Please write to Tony Holmes via e-mail at: tony.holmes@osprey-jets.freeserve.co.uk or tonyholmes67@yahoo.co.uk

CONTENTS

INTRODUCTION

Two F-14As from VF-41 gave the Tomcat its combat debut as a bomber when they dropped ordnance on an ammunition dump in Bosnia-Herzegovina on 5 September 1995 as part of Operation *Deliberate Force*. Lacking any way to target their laser-guided bombs (LGBs), the Tomcat crews relied on Hornets to designate the dump for them. Six years later, the 'Black Aces' were once again in the vanguard of combat operations involving the F-14, although by now the Tomcat had evolved into naval aviation's premier precision strike platform. The veteran jet's effectiveness in this mission would be shown over and over again during US-led Operation *Enduring Freedom* (OEF), the first conflict in the Global War on Terror.

As a follow-on volume to my 2005 book *Osprey Combat Aircraft 52 – US Navy Tomcat units of Operation Iraqi Freedom* (OIF), this volume in the same series examines the exploits of the F-14 squadrons that took the fight to the Taleban and al-Qaeda in land-locked Afghanistan in 2001-03.

Acknowledgements

Many naval aviators who flew the Tomcat in combat in OEF have made valuable contributions to this book. Thanks to the personnel who man the US Navy's Chief of Naval Information (CHINFO) News Desk in the Pentagon, I was given clearance to interview Tomcat aircrew at NAS Lemoore, NAS Fallon and NAS Oceana. I would like to take this opportunity to thank CHINFO's Capt John Fleming, COMNAVAIRLANT's Deputy Public Affairs Officer (PAO) Mike Maus, NSAWC PAO Lt Cdr Karla Olson and NAS Lemoore PAO Dennis McGrath for assisting me during my visits to these facilities. Thanks also to Capt Andy Lewis and Lt Col Karl Brandt of VFA-106 for their assistance in arranging interviews with naval aviators in their command.

Fellow Osprey authors Peter Mersky and Robert 'Boom' Powell, as well as retired naval aviator Neil Jennings, provided generous hospitality during my 2006 road trip. Thanks also to Dave Parsons, David F Brown, Brian Marbrey and other members of the F-14 Tomcat Association Forum, as well as Rodger Kelly and Richard Siudak of the ANA's No 55 Sqn in Western Australia, for their factual and photographic contributions.

Finally, this book could not have been written without input from the following pilots, naval flight officers, Intelligence Officers and Chief Warrant Officers (2007 ranks given) from the following units, whose OIF experiences, and photographs, fill this volume;

CVW-8 – Capt David Newland and Lt Cdr Bill Lind
CVW-11 – Capt Chuck Wright and Lt Carlos Ortiz
CVW-14 – Lt Cdr Jim Muse
VF-11 – Capt John Aquilino, Cdr Chris Chope and Lt Brian Vanyo
VF-14 – Capt Bruce Fecht, Cdr Will Pennington, Cdr Jake Ellzey, Cdr Marcell Padilla, Lt Cdr Van Kizer, Lt Mike Bradley and Lt Thomas Bodine
VF-41 – Capt Brian Gawne, Capt Pat Cleary, Cdr Scott Butler, Cdr David Lobdell, Lt Cdr John Kelly, Lt Cdr Marcus Lopez and Lt Shawn Price
VF-102 – Cdr John Cummings, Cdr Tom Eberhard, Cdr Scott Guimond, Lt Cdr Andrew Hayes, Lt Cdr Chad Mingo, Lt Cdr Derek Nalwajko, Lt Dan Quinn, Lt Sara Stires and CWO3 Carleton Roe
VF-103 – Cdr Lou Schager and Lt Mike Meason
VF-143 – Lt Cdr Brian Fitting, Lt Cdr William Mallory and Lt Joseph Greentree
VF-211 – Cdr Nick Dienna, Lt Cdr Shaun Swartz, Lt Dan Buchar, Lt Mario Duarte, Lt Mitch McCallister and Lt Kevin Robb
VF-213 – Cdr Chip King, Capt Anthony Giaini, Cdr Michael Peterson, Lt Cdr Brian Hodges, Lt Cdr Andrew Mickley, Lt Cdr John Saccomando, Lt Cdr Geoffrey Vickers, Lt Nate Bailey, Lt Tony Toma and CWO3 Michael Lavoie

Tony Holmes, Sevenoaks, Kent, October 2007

BUILD-UP TO WAR

At 0846 hrs on the morning of 11 September 2001, American Airlines Flight 11 – a Boeing 767 – from Boston, Massachusetts, flew into the north tower of the World Trade Center in downtown Manhattan. On the other side of the world, the personnel of Carrier Air Wing (CVW) 8, aboard USS *Enterprise* (CVN-65), were watching the aftermath of this seemingly tragic accident in real time. The veteran aircraft carrier was well into the final weeks of what had originally been scheduled as a routine six-month deployment. Indeed, 48 hours earlier, it had handed over responsibility for patrolling Iraq as part of the US Navy's commitment to Operation *Southern Watch* (OSW) to USS *Carl Vinson* (CVN-70), with CVW-11 embarked. Having chopped out of Fifth Fleet control, the 'Big E' was heading home.

Following five weeks of intensive combat operations performing the OSW mission, CVW-8 was enjoying its first no-fly day in more than a month on the 11th. However, for CVW-11, it was business as usual, as CVN-70 sailed west towards the Middle East. Just two days out of port, following a spell of rest & recreation in Singapore, the air wing was getting back into the swing of things with some routine training missions. The carrier was just preparing for a recovery cycle when the north tower was hit. One of the pilots in the landing pattern was the commanding officer of VF-213, Cdr Chip King;

'I trapped back aboard just minutes after the first airliner went in. My gunner, CWO3 Michael Lavoie, met me with a host of young sailors at the jet immediately after I had taxied out of the landing area, and he

Three F-14As and two F/A-18Cs sit chained down to the deck over CVN-65's bow catapult two in August 2001. CVW-8 was in the middle of its five-week commitment to OSW when this photograph was taken. Climbing away from the carrier in phase five afterburner at the start of yet another lengthy mission over southern Iraq is VF-41's 'Fast Eagle 104' (BuNo 158630). 'We dropped just three GBU-12s and four GBU-16s during our short time manning the OSW station', VF-41 CO Cdr Brian Gawne recalled. 'Only five of the eleven strikes we flew into Iraq were executed. Our targets were what we dubbed the "Frankenstein" SAM sites, which the Iraqis had modified so as to make them difficult to detect – the SA-2 and SA-3s had been fitted with different types of seeker heads, and the launchers would be regularly moved around'. In OEF, LTS-equipped 'Fast Eagle 104' (nicknamed *Delores* by VF-41's Maintenance Master Chief, AVCM Randy Bradley) would expend 24 LGBs (*US Navy*)

told me that an aircraft had just hit the World Trade Center. We made it down to the ready room in time to see a second airliner slam into the south tower on CNN. At that moment I knew we would be involved in America's response to these horrendous acts of terror.'

Several hundred miles northwest of CVN-70, the naval aviators of VF-14 and VF-41 were unwinding following weeks of patrolling over southern Iraq. They were looking forward to a well-earned port call in Cape Town, South Africa – a destination never previously visited by a US aircraft carrier. Amongst those aboard the vessel observing the world-changing events in New York unfold that Tuesday afternoon was Cdr Brian Gawne, CO of VF-41;

'CVW-8 had conducted its fifth, and last, OSW strike on the night of 9 September, when a mobile Iraqi air-search radar had been destroyed. The *Enterprise* battle group had then exited the Northern Arabian Gulf (NAG) the following day after we had completed our turnover with CVW-11. When CVN-65 cleared the Straits of Hormuz, it was like a celebration. The temperature had dropped to a reasonable level, and *Enterprise* was sailing south towards Cape Town. We were scheduled to cross the Equator, which was a rare experience for an East Coast carrier.

'Our junior officers were on the Internet trying to set up fishing trips and find the best Irish pubs. There was a definite sense of accomplishment in CVW-8 – we were on our way home, we had performed successfully during actual strikes, and we had not lost a single aircraft. Within VF-41, we had already shifted our mindset from flying Tomcats over Iraq to commencing our post-deployment homeport change from NAS Oceana, Virginia, to NAS Lemoore, California, and subsequent transition to the F/A-18F Super Hornet.

'With 11 September 2001 being a no-fly day, most of us had enjoyed a rare sleep in. Having done some work in my stateroom, I finally walked into the ready room just before 1600 hrs, and was immediately told that an aeroplane had flown into the north tower of the World Trade Center. The boat had had a good satellite television link with home for most of the cruise, and when the first aeroplane hit the building, the word went through the carrier immediately.

'Less than five minutes after I had entered the ready room, I watched in horror as the Boeing 767 of United Airlines Flight 175 from Boston struck the south tower. Like everyone else in uniform, I knew that two aircraft hitting the World Trade Center was no accident.'

Elsewhere on the ship, CVN-65's CO, and former F-14 pilot, Capt James Winnefeld, had been watching CNN when the second airliner slammed into the south tower;

'Right then I thought "we're not going home". It was only a matter of hours before we were ordered to turn around.'

Capt Winnefeld immediately informed the ship's crew of this change of plans via the vessel's 1MC (shipboard public address system), and the 90,000-ton vessel turned through 180 degrees and headed back north. 'We knew that we still had work to do on the cruise', Cdr Gawne recalled.

Prior to CVN-65 changing course, Tomcat RIO and CVW-8 Strike Operations Officer Lt Cdr Bill Lind had been instructed by his Air Wing Commander, Capt Dave Mercer, to 'immediately stand up a slew of alert fighters, to include aircraft spotted on the catapults with crews aboard –

our highest state of readiness. Things then began to get hectic, as we arranged for ordnance to be broken out and loaded and aircrew and aircraft to be identified for launching on retaliatory strikes. To add a dramatic exclamation point to these efforts, we also felt *Enterprise* heel over in a sharp 180-degree turn and head north at top speed. Chances were that the people responsible for the attacks on Manhattan and the Pentagon that we were watching on our television screens weren't from South Africa. We were headed back to the Straits of Hormuz'.

Several hundred miles to the southeast, off the tip of India, the crew of *Carl Vinson* had also seen these devastating attacks. They too would be ordered to alter their ship's course for the Northern Arabian Sea, rather than the NAG.

Back at NAS Oceana, home of Commander, Fighter Wing US Atlantic Fleet, four Tomcat squadrons that would subsequently participate in the forthcoming Global War on Terror in Afghanistan were also caught up in the events of 11 September. F-14B-equipped VF-102, assigned to CVW-1, had all but completed its pre-cruise work-ups and was scheduled to embark in USS *Theodore Roosevelt* (CVN-71) for a six-month deployment on the 21st of that month. The departure date for the cruise would duly be brought forward by 48 hours.

The 11 F-14As of CVW-9's VF-211 were actually en route to NAS Fallon, Nevada, for the air wing's all-important three-week-long strike training phase when the 11 September attacks occurred. The unit was immediately turned around and sent back to Oceana, before eventually making it to Fallon 48 hours later. CVW-9 would subsequently complete a truncated work-up cycle and head for the Northern Arabian Sea aboard USS *John C Stennis* (CVN-74) on 12 November, some two months earlier than originally planned.

Although CVW-7's VF-11 and VF-143 were still in the early stages of their work-ups on 11 September, the units' response to the attacks was immediate. North American Aerospace Defense Command (NORAD) had contacted the Navy after the south tower was hit asking for its help in securing the airspace over the eastern seaboard. Second Fleet immediately ordered all available ships to set sail from its bases at Norfolk, Virginia, and Mayport, Florida, as quickly as possible. One of the vessels departing the latter naval yard was CVW-7's carrier USS *John F Kennedy* (CV-67).

Ashore, the air wing had been ordered to embark its F-14Bs aboard CV-67 and send its two squadrons of F/A-18Cs to USS *George Washington* (CVN-73), which had left Norfolk on a post-maintenance shakedown cruise without any aircraft embarked just prior to the attacks.

VF-143's Lt(jg) Joseph Greentree subsequently flew several missions in support of the NORAD-controlled sea shield that had been hastily established off the coast of New York;

'11 September 2001 was scheduled to have been the first day of our COMPTUEX (Composite Training Unit Exercise) aboard "JFK". The carrier was scheduled to sail from Mayport at noon and then embark CVW-7 as it neared the Virginia coast. Everything changed following the attacks on New York and Washington, D.C., however. For the first 72 hours that VF-11 and VF-143 were embarked in *Kennedy*, we flew round-the-clock Combat Air Patrols (CAPs) up and down the eastern seaboard. The skies remained eerily empty during our time manning

CAPs, with all civilian air traffic having been grounded. After three days, Second Fleet told us to abandon these CAP missions and commence the COMPTUEX instead, so the Hornets returned to "JFK" from "GW".'

RESPONSE

Within hours of the World Trade Center and the Pentagon being hit, US intelligence services had identified Osama Bin Laden's al-Qaeda terrorist group as the perpetrators of these atrocities. Aboard *Carl Vinson*, VF-213's Intelligence Officer, Lt(jg) Nate Bailey, was monitoring signals traffic being picked up by the ship in the aftermath of the attacks;

'I was sat in CVN-70's Carrier Intelligence Center (CVIC) when the airliners hit the twin towers. Soon after the attacks, I went over and spoke with the ship's Intelligence Collection Manager, who had noticed that nearly every national intelligence collection asset available was shifting its priority to Afghanistan. Almost immediately the "requirements deck" focused on Afghanistan too, and it became clear that CVW-11's focus for the rest of the deployment would be on this land-locked country as well.'

Although nowhere near as familiar a target as southern Iraq, Afghanistan was not a complete stranger to American air strikes, having been hit by Tomahawk Land Attack Missiles (TLAMs) fired from warships of the US Navy's Fifth Fleet on 20 August 1998. This attack, authorised by President Bill Clinton, had targeted al-Qaeda's Zhawar Kili Al-Badr base camp, training facility and support complex in the eastern mountains of Afghanistan following the bombing of the American embassies in Kenya and Tanzania 13 days earlier.

The Central Intelligence Agency (CIA) and the Federal Bureau of Investigation (FBI) had been monitoring the movements of Osama Bin Laden prior to the embassy attacks, and after the TLAMs had failed to get him, they started following the Saudi terrorist around Afghanistan, trying to work out ways to deliver a killer blow. The CIA's small force of Predator unmanned aerial vehicles (UAVs), based in neighbouring Uzbekistan, played a key role in tracking al-Qaeda during this period.

A plan to remove the ruling Taleban government from power in the country was also devised, although the question of Pakistani sovereignty restricting aircraft overflights from the Northern Arabian Sea posed a thorny problem that could not be solved at the time. As Central Command (CENTCOM) staff officer Vice Admiral David Nichols told Rebecca Grant, author of *Battle-Tested – Carrier Aviation in Afghanistan and Iraq*, when interviewed in 2004;

'There was plenty of political will on the part of the Clinton administration to get Osama, but there was not much appetite for political and diplomatic risk, and changing the way we did business in that part of the world.'

Their pre-flight walkaround completed, a pilot and RIO from VF-213 settle themselves into the cockpit of their F-14D prior to flying a vital TARPS mission along the Afghan-Pakistan border in early October 2001. CVW-11 staff officer and Tomcat RIO Lt Carlos Ortiz routinely flew photo-reconnaissance missions both before and during OIF with VF-213. 'Going against the military adage of "never do a shitty job well", I found my niche flying TARPS sorties in OEF – I had flown countless such missions during my tour with VF-143 some years earlier', he recalled. 'Photo-recce was never popular in the Tomcat community, as crews preferred to be conducting more offensive missions that involved dropping bombs on targets or searching for enemy aircraft to shoot down.

'As long as you didn't miss your waypoints, flying a TARPS mission was not too difficult a job. We quickly realised that there were few features on the ground that we could use to help guide us when overflying Afghanistan, so we relied almost exclusively on GPS. VF-213's jets were also equipped with Link-16 JTIDS (Joint Tactical Information Distribution System), which gave the crew GPS capabilities. However, I always relied on my own personal hand-held Garmin Pilot III GPS, which I had been using for a number of years prior to OEF – it was my own safety blanket' (*US Navy*)

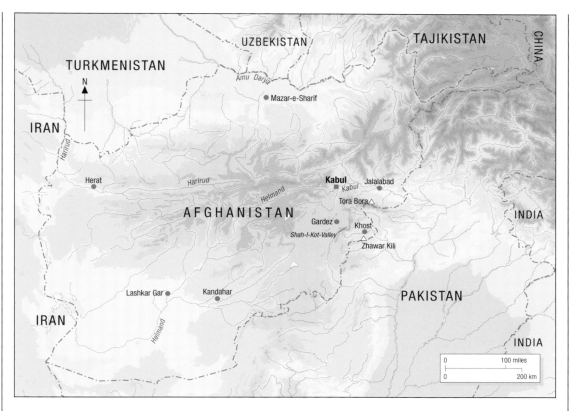

US intelligence on Taleban and al-Qaeda targets in Afghanistan was sketchy at best prior to 11 September 2001. However, a fuller picture of the key military sites that needed to be taken out to ensure regime change in the country was hastily built up in the short time between the World Trade Center and Pentagon attacks and the start of OEF. The attention of virtually all national intelligence-gathering assets, both manned and unmanned, was focused on Afghanistan's key cities of Kabul, Kandahar, Gardez, Herat and Mazar-e-Sharif. Terrorist training camps, including those in Zhawar Kili and Tora Bora, were also picked out as targets, as were SAM and AAA sites, air bases, military barracks and tank/armoured personnel carrier (APC)/vehicle parks (*Copyright Osprey Publishing*)

Emboldened by the success of the embassy bombings, al-Qaeda struck again on 12 October 2000 when a small boat packed with explosives was detonated by its crew while alongside the destroyer USS *Cole* (DDG-67). The vessel was being refuelled in the Yemeni port of Aden at the time, and 17 sailors lost their lives. The US government again came close to ordering a TLAM strike in retaliation, but the CIA urged President Clinton to call it off at the last minute because Osama Bin Laden's precise location was unknown at the time. A large-scale bombing campaign of all known terrorists' camps and a full-scale invasion of Afghanistan were also contemplated, but neither were deemed to be 'feasible without a finding of al-Qaeda responsibility for the *Cole*', concluded President Clinton in his autobiography, *My Life*.

It did not take long for al-Qaeda to be directly linked to the 11 September 2001 attacks, however. Just hours after the towers had come down, a Senate Intelligence Committee in Washington, D.C. had been told about electronic intercepts that revealed representatives affiliated with Osama Bin Laden reporting that they had hit two targets. And three weeks prior to the attack, Bin Laden had told a London-based Arabic magazine of a pending 'unprecedented attack, a very big one' against American interests.

With US forces at Defense Condition 3 – their highest alert state since the Yom Kippur War of October 1973 – US Secretary of State Colin Powell gave a clear indication of how the Bush administration would respond to what the president had described as 'the first war of the 21st century'. On 12 September he stressed that the United States would 'hold accountable those countries that provide support and facilities to these kinds of terrorist groups. We will be directing our efforts not only against terrorists, but also against those that harbour and provide haven and support for terrorism'.

War with al-Qaeda, and the Taleban regime that provided the much-reviled organisation with a base for its training camps in Afghanistan, now seemed inevitable. As if to confirm this, Deputy Secretary of Defense Paul Wolfowitz commented on 14 September that 'It's not just simply a matter of capturing people and holding them accountable, but removing the sanctuaries, removing the support systems, ending states who sponsor terrorism. We will wage a campaign, not a single action'.

PLAN FOR WAR

Less than three weeks after the 11 September attacks, carrier-based aircraft would be in the vanguard of a joint operation to remove the Taleban from power and destroy the organisational infrastructure that al-Qaeda had established in Afghanistan. The framework for this campaign, which was eventually codenamed Operation *Enduring Freedom* (OEF), was far from being in place when Secretary of Defense Donald Rumsfeld directed the commander of CENTCOM, Army Gen Tommy Franks, to start preparing 'credible military options' on 12 September.

With its responsibility for US security interests in 25 nations stretching from the Horn of Africa through the Arabian Gulf region and into Central Asia, CENTCOM would be charged with running OEF. Gen Franks immediately asked the secretary of defense for a week to ten days to come up with a course of action for the Afghanistan campaign. 'We had al-Qaeda and Taleban target sets in-country, and plans to strike those targets with TLAMs and manned bombers, but CENTCOM had not developed a plan for conventional ground operations in Afghanistan, or for access agreements with bordering nations', Gen Franks revealed in his autobiography, *American Soldier.*

Initially, CENTCOM's senior planners, led by Franks, favoured a multi-pronged land attack on Afghanistan via helicopter, with Pakistan being used as a vital staging area. However, Pakistan was reluctant to provide such access for US military assets, and even if approval had been granted, the force estimates that CENTCOM was calling for would have taken too long to amass in-theatre. President Bush was keen to strike back as swiftly as possible, so in order to do this Donald Rumsfeld cut the timeline for when OEF was to start. The number of troops and aircraft committed to the campaign were reduced accordingly, thus ruling out the possibility of a fully blown ground war.

CENTCOM was forced to look at other ways to ensure regime change, and it decided that strengthening the opposition forces that had been fighting the Taleban for years was the only way ahead. Prevented from putting large numbers of troops on the ground in-country, CENTCOM would have to rely on air power and Special Operations Forces (SOF) teams when providing support for anti-Taleban fighters in Afghanistan.

The opposition forces had strongholds in the northern, western and southern regions of the country, with the Taleban having seized control of the remaining 80 percent of Afghanistan in a bitter civil war that had raged since 1996. Far from presenting themselves as a cohesive force, the opposition groups were aligned along ethnic and religious lines. The most powerful of these groups was the Northern Alliance, which held the mountains near the old Afghan-Soviet border. With several smaller groups included within its power base, the Northern Alliance was estimated to control some 15,000 fighters.

Al-Qaeda clearly recognised the threat posed by the Northern Alliance, for it had assassinated the group's leader, Ahmad Shah Masood, in a suicide bomb attack on 9 September 2001. The CIA had also valued what Masood and his fighters were trying to do in Afghanistan, having covertly supported him for several years.

The Northern Alliance was now identified by CENTCOM and the Bush administration as being the best bet for expeditious regime change in Afghanistan, and Donald Rumsfeld clearly indicated this when he participated in a 'meet the press' session on 1 October;

'Unconventional approaches are much more likely and more appropriate than the typical conventional approach of armies and navies and air forces. There's no question but that there are any number of people in Afghanistan – tribes in the south and Northern Alliance in the north – that oppose the Taleban, and clearly we need to recognise the value they bring to this anti-terrorist, anti-Taleban effort, and where possible find ways to assist them.'

Those 'ways' would take the form of firepower courtesy of CENTCOM's Central Command Air Forces (CENTAF), which during the early stages of OEF was provided in the main by carrier-based strike aircraft in the Northern Arabian Sea. And naval aviators would have to play the pivotal role in the first campaign of the Global War on Terror because the only other tactical aircraft that could reach landlocked Afghanistan were long-endurance B-52H, B-1B and B-2A bombers. This trio of USAF 'heavies' could not achieve air superiority over Afghanistan, however, and CENTCOM needed this if it was to provide humanitarian relief via C-17 airdrops, as well as the insertion/extraction of SOF teams. Again, only the Navy's Hornets and Tomcats were close enough to Afghanistan to ensure the fighter coverage CENTCOM required.

Yet even naval aircraft could not reach targets in Afghanistan if Pakistan refused to grant US warplanes clearance to pass through its sovereign airspace – the Pakistani coastline along the Northern Arabian Sea provided the most direct route to Afghanistan from Fifth Fleet aircraft carriers sailing some 70 miles due south of Karachi.

As part of the Bush administration's drive to globalise the fight against terror, it had made determined efforts to assemble a broad coalition of nations prior to committing its armed forces to all-out war. NATO was called to arms by the invoking of the mutual defence clause by the North Atlantic Council for the first time in its 52-year history. Numerous other countries also offered their support, including Russia, which in turn pressured Pakistan to provide intelligence and logistical support.

The United Nations resolution condemning the 11 September attack, which called for 'urgent international cooperation to prevent and eradicate acts of terrorism', also helped convince Pakistan to open its skies to US military aircraft, and make bases available for the staging of SOF and combat search and rescue (CSAR) operations. It was long-standing US practice that no aerial attacks could be authorised without a viable CSAR capability in place beforehand.

Tajikistan and Uzbekistan, which were northern neighbours of Afghanistan, also offered bases for use by SOF, logistical and tanker units (but not, crucially, USAF F-15E and F-16 fighter wings) on 21 September, and Donald Rumsfeld gave the order to send men and materiel to these locations shortly thereafter.

The final piece in the CENTCOM puzzle when it came to running a sustained aerial campaign in OEF was the Saudi government's approval for CENTAF to use its newly-built Combined Air Operations Center (CAOC) at Prince Sultan Air Base, dubbed PSAB. The nerve centre that controlled all CENTAF assets in the region, the facility had only opened in early 2001 following the CAOC's move from Riyadh. Packed with communication equipment that pulled in both VHF and satellite signals via nine-metre receiver dishes and displayed all this information on huge data walls, the CAOC was staffed by personnel from Joint Task Force - Southwest Asia posted in from all branches of the US armed forces. Officers from Coalition allies such as Britain and Australia could also be found working in the teams that ran the CAOC's operations floor.

By September 2001, the CAOC had been controlling air assets conducting OSW overfights of southern Iraq for almost ten years. It therefore had plenty of experience handling packages of strike aircraft – supported by tankers, AWACS and electronic warfare platforms – operating over enemy territory.

With the command and control assets in place, permission to overfly Pakistan all but secured and airfields in Tajikistan and Uzbekistan now available for vital tanker support and as SOF staging posts, CENTCOM began planning how best to employ the TACAIR units aboard *Enterprise* and *Carl Vinson* in the Northern Arabian Sea. The F-14s and F/A-18s would initially be charged with gaining air superiority, after which they would attack key Taleban and al-Qaeda targets such as air bases, SAM sites, AAA batteries, barracks, ammunition dumps, tank/APC/truck parks and terrorist training camps. They would also have to provide flexible precision bombing capability for Afghan opposition forces operating under SOF guidance in their efforts to defeat the Taleban.

Only limited USAF TACAIR support would be available to CENTCOM during the early stages of OEF, as the closest F-15Es and F-16Cs were based in Kuwait and Qatar, respectively.

Gen Franks briefed President Bush on CENTCOM's plan for OEF on 21 September, emphasising the importance placed on early air strikes against fixed targets and then the sustained campaign of flexible close air support for Afghan opposition forces, aided by small, but numerous, SOF teams. The general

VF-14's 'Tophatter 200' (BuNo 162698) and '204' (BuNo 161863) return to marshal at the end of a training mission in late September. 'VF-14 and VF-41 – and the air wing as a whole – maintained a surprisingly robust flight schedule between 11 September and 7 October, when OEF commenced', explained 'Black Aces' RIO, and squadron maintenance officer, Lt Cdr Scott Butler. 'We were flying a lot harder than I would have expected if you had wanted to be grooming elderly jets for combat. Our F-14s had been flown a lot over the previous five-and-a-half months of the deployment leading up to OEF, and they deserved a break.

'Although CVW-8 had the oldest Tomcats in the fleet, both VF-14 and VF-41 were lucky enough to have the best maintenance departments in the fleet too. As maintenance officer in charge of the sailors in my unit, I know just how hard they worked to keep the 11 jets we had serviceable during the final hectic weeks of cruise. The long OEF missions came at the end of what had already been a full deployment for our aircraft. However, once we knew that we were going to war, both units routinely undertook multiple eight- and nine-hour missions per day as we prepared for the marathon sorties that would become synonymous with OEF.

'We did a lot of Unit Level Training, a number of escort flights for transports carrying humanitarian aid and some tanker proving sorties to validate our proposed route planning and fuel burn calculations prior to OEF commencing' (*VF-14*)

told the president that carrier aircraft could start striking targets within 24 hours if so directed, but Franks urged his commander-in-chief to wait a further two weeks while the USAF got its tankers and AWACS assets bedded down at airfields in the CENTCOM theatre of operations. CSAR and SOF bases in Pakistan also needed to be established. President Bush agreed to delay the start of OEF until 7 October.

Two days prior to this meeting taking place, *Theodore Roosevelt* had departed Norfolk naval yard with CVW-1 embarked. Amongst the four TACAIR units controlled by the air wing was F-14B-equipped VF-102, and one of the squadron's junior officers told the Author;

'After several days getting all the pilots in CVW-1 suitably deck qualified for both day and night operations in the Virginia Capes exercise area, CVN-71 sped due east across the Atlantic into the Mediterranean. Here, we put the brakes on for a few days and participated in the opening stages of Exercise *Bright Star* with Egypt. The rumour circulating around the ship at the time was that our admiral (Rear Admiral Mark Fitzgerald) had been instructed to keep an eye on the political situation in Syria and Egypt in the wake of the 9/11 attacks, keeping a carrier in the eastern Mediterranean while *Enterprise* and *Carl Vinson* kicked OEF off. Much to our frustration, we stayed in the area for almost two weeks, before sailing through the Suez Canal.'

While VF-102 and the rest of CVW-1 were heading for the Northern Arabian Sea, CVW-8 and CVW-11 had been busy preparing their crews for the conflict to come. Prior to departing on cruise, neither air wing had given much thought to flying combat missions over Afghanistan, as VF-213's Lt(jg) Nate Bailey recalled;

'Combat operations in Afghanistan were something we had not even considered. Our primary focus, both during our work-ups and in our voyage from San Diego across the Pacific and Indian Oceans, was our role in the NAG, not with a land-locked country in Central Asia. In fact, as part of our jobs, everyone in CVW-8's Intel department was tasked with being a Subject Matter Expert (SME) on different countries/issues in the Western Pacific and Middle East areas. Reflecting the threat level associated with Afghanistan pre-9/11, its SME was a very junior sailor. However, by the end of September, we had all become SMEs on Afghanistan. While there wasn't very much up-to-date information out

CH-46Ds from HC-11 deliver 'bombs, bullets and beans' to CVN-65 from the Military Sealift Command fast combat support ship USNS *Arctic* (T-AOE 8) during a vertical replenishment (VERTREP) in the Northern Arabian Sea on the eve of OEF. Such restocking of munitions, spare parts and foodstuffs would occur every few days once combat commenced, with the vessel's ammunition magazines, in particular, being rapidly depleted as CVW-8 worked its way through the CAOC's target hit list (*US Navy*)

there on the state of the country's air defences, we would analyse anything we could get – old Soviet accounts of their campaigns and lessons learned, imagery of fixed SAM sites, history of the Taleban and al-Qaeda's presence in Afghanistan, etc.'

As part of the overall mission planning that was now taking place in earnest in the CAOC, both air wings sent senior naval aviators to PSAB to represent them during the drafting phase of the Master Air Attack Plan (MAAP) for OEF. VF-213's executive officer, Cdr Anthony Giaini, was one of those involved;

'Just four days after the 9/11 attacks, I found myself strapped into a C-2 COD bound for PSAB as one of two officers from CVW-11 sent to the CAOC – along with representatives from CVW-8 – to help CENTAF plan the air campaign for what would become OEF.

'I'd like to say that this plan was quickly written and agreed upon, but it wasn't. We lacked many things, and intelligence and guidance as to the aims and objectives of the campaign took a while to firm up. The result was more than a dozen draft plans that eventually resulted in what we executed on 7 October. The plan itself reflected some hard political realities, as for OEF to succeed, we would require the support of everyone from very shaky friends to our traditional and closest allies. The key nations for us were Pakistan (whose territory we would have to cross) and Britain, who, luckily for us, had an exercise underway in Oman at the time, and the RAF had big wing tankers already in-theatre. Frankly, we couldn't have fought OEF without the help of both nations.'

Heading up the Navy mission in the CAOC pre-war was Capt Dave Newland, DCAG of CVW-8. Destined to later fly a number of combat missions as a RIO with both VF-14 and VF-41, he remembers 'spending many long days and nights planning what was to become OEF'.

One of Capt Newland's staff officers back aboard CVN-65 was fellow Tomcat RIO Lt Cdr Bill Lind, who recalled receiving the MAAP in its original form in late September;

'Our getting this plan was fairly dramatic. CAG (Capt Dave Mercer), DCAG (Capt Newland), the COs of the fighter (VF-14 and VF-41), strike fighter (VFA-15 and VFA-87) and electronic warfare (VAQ-141) squadrons, the CAG Operations Officer and I were ushered into a secure area of the CVIC by one of our intelligence guys. We were required to sign a multitude of forms, after which we were given sealed packets. These were opened in unison once the paperwork was in order – a scene that reminded me of any number of late-night war movies I watched as a kid. I was humbled to be a part of this crowd.

'The plan was as large as it was audacious. This was to be no pinprick retaliatory strike. This was a campaign centred on air power. Providing me with yet another sense of the unreal, if this plan were to come to fruition, it would see US naval air power let off the leash like no time since World War 2. We would have full tanker support over Afghanistan, as well as AWACS coverage from overhead Pakistan, and the target list eliminated not only the limited command and control nodes of the Taleban and al-Qaeda, but just about every piece of military gear and potential military site in the country.

'As exciting as it was to review the plan and charts from my "secret-squirrel" package, a career of half-measures in response to any number

The eight TARPS jets assigned to VF-41 and VF-213 were heavily tasked by CENTCOM via the CAOC in the build-up to OEF. The canoe-like photo-reconnaissance pod was typically secured to the aircraft's rear right Phoenix missile station five, and although weighing in at 1760 lbs, it imposed few performance penalties on the F-14 other than restricting the carriage of missiles/bombs on the aft tunnel stations. 'Our TARPS missions were a critical component to the overall intelligence collection efforts run out of the CAOC', recalled VF-213's intelligence officer, Lt(jg) Nate Bailey. The value of these missions became even greater once the SOF elements learned of this capability.

'As the mission progressed, intelligence elements embedded with SOF units would work with us directly in supporting SOF operations. For a capability that was on its last legs, TARPS was used nearly every day that VF-213 was committed to OEF, and it was highly sought after to support some very important operations. Since Afghanistan was not an intelligence collection focus point prior to 9/11, the F-14's TARPS capability filled key gaps in providing situational awareness on the enemy's lines of communication, cities and military sites and encampments' (*US Navy*)

of situations and outright depredations towards the United States throughout the 1990s made me wonder how much of this we'd be allowed to execute. I'd get the chance to find out very soon.'

While planners in the CAOC had been busy creating the MAAP, naval aviators had also been making preparations for war at unit level. They were actively working on rough plans to ensure, once the final MAAP was released to them, that the CAOC had allocated enough fuel, adequate AWACS control, EW support and the right ordnance for the expected targets.

Aboard *Carl Vinson*, Lt(jg) Nate Bailey was also busy briefing VF-213 crews on the threats that they could expect to face once OEF commenced;

'The fact of the matter was that while the air-to-air threat – at most fewer than 50 MiG-21s and Su-22s – was not great compared to other potential adversaries, the surface-to-air threat was still a bit of an unknown. We knew that the Taleban had fixed SAM sites around their main strategic centres, but the proficiency of the operators was certainly a question. In my opinion, the more immediate threat was posed by the heavy-calibre AAA pieces that would be located at higher elevations (mountain passes, etc.). This tactic was observed during the Soviet occupation, and we briefed that we could expect to see the same thing.

'Besides briefing the threat, the other key part of my job as an intelligence officer pre-OEF was to support the targeting process. For the first phase of the air war, the CAOC produced a prioritised target list. The Intel folks on the carrier then broke the list down into target folders – working closely with members of the air wing strike teams – in order to provide the best situational awareness of the target area, as well as desired ordnance impact specifics.

'Targeting, in my opinion, is certainly the most "satisfying", and yet most sober, part of being an intelligence officer in this environment. We had guidance to be aggressive and "take down the Taleban" and yet the

specifics to that often fell to junior officers. Of all the target nominations I submitted – from TARPS (Tactical Aerial Reconnaissance Pod System) imagery, for example – to the CAOC, all were approved. While we were aggressive, we also realised that we were dealing with real people on the ground. A surreal balance to be sure.'

TOMCAT TO THE FORE

The 33 Tomcats shared between the three fighter squadrons in the Northern Arabian Sea at the start of OEF would play a pivotal role in the execution of the air campaign over Afghanistan. By October 2001, the F-14 had shown just how well it could perform as a precision bomber during combat over Iraq in Operation *Desert Fox* in December 1998, Operation *Allied Force* in Kosovo and Serbia in the spring of 1999 and during the latter years of OSW. Arguably the aircraft's 'finest hour' in US Navy service would come during OEF, when the Tomcat's firepower, targeting systems and, most importantly of all, range were used to their maximum potential by well-trained naval aviators thoroughly familiar with the aircraft's warfighting capabilities.

How the F-14's fortunes had changed during the course of the previous decade leading up to OEF. Although the aircraft had proven itself to be a valuable reconnaissance platform during Operation *Desert Storm* in 1991, the Tomcat had by then become a victim of the very Cold War strategies that had seen it created as a fighter interceptor and exclusively tasked with repelling waves of missile-carrying Soviet bombers hell bent on sinking Navy carriers. Lacking the systems to allow their crews to comply with the strict rules of engagement (ROE) that would have allowed them to autonomously engage Iraqi air targets using only their onboard sensors, F-14 units were reliant on controlling platforms such as USAF E-3 AWACS aircraft for a clearance to fire. Left to fly combat air patrols over the NAG hundreds of miles south of the real action in Iraq, F-14 crews claimed only a single Mi-8 helicopter shot down during the entire war.

The post-*Desert Storm* years were bleak ones for the Navy's fighter community, with swingeing budget cuts seeing ten frontline Tomcat units decommissioned due to the jet's limited mission capability and astronomical flight-hour costs. Yet just when it looked as if the F-14's ocean-going days were numbered, a reprieve came thanks to the acceler-ated demise of another Grumman 'Ironworks' product. The all-weather, long-range A-6 Intruder bomber was hastily taken out of service in the mid-1990s, again due to high maintenance costs and the supposed evaporation of its mission in the post-Cold War world.

With the Intruder on the verge of retirement, and the Tomcat seemingly following in its footsteps, the Navy now found itself facing a shortage of tactical carrier aircraft to fulfil its global 'policing' mission.

When the F-14 was developed in the late 1960s, Grumman had built the jet with the capability to drop bombs, although the Navy had not specified this mission requirement. For the first two decades of its fleet life, the Tomcat had been operated almost exclusively as a fighter, with the photo-reconnaissance role only being reluctantly adopted by fleet squadrons in the early 1980s following the development of TARPS. Threatened by wholesale decommissioning in the wake of *Desert Storm*, the fighter community looked to diversify in order to survive, and seeing that the all-weather precision bombing role once performed by the A-6 was now vacant, a push was made to pair the Tomcat up with some form of bolt-on targeting pod.

Experimentation with gravity bombs hung beneath Tomcats had taken place as early as November 1987, although senior naval officers realised that the F-14 would not be a viable fighter/attack platform without a precision weapons delivery capability. Little funding was available to develop an all-new system for the jet, so an 'off-the-shelf' targeting pod was acquired thanks to the securing of modest financing through the lobbying of Commander, Naval Air Forces Atlantic in the autumn of 1994. The equipment chosen was the combat-proven AAQ-14 LANTIRN (Low Altitude Navigation and Targeting InfraRed for Night) pod, developed for the F-15E by Martin Marietta.

Working with a tiny budget, the Tomcat community, ably assisted by a clutch of defence contractors, integrated the digital pod with the analogue F-14A/B, and by March 1995 a test aircraft was dropping laser-guided bombs (LGBs) with the aid of LANTIRN. The results from this early evaluation were stunning, with the Tomcat crew obtaining better infra-red imagery, and bomb accuracy, than the similarly-equipped USAF F-15E Strike Eagle and F-16C Fighting Falcon due to the RIO's ability to locate targets on his large Programmable Tactical Information Display (PTID). The USAF strike aircraft, by contrast, only had small Multi-Function Displays (MFDs).

On 14 June 1996 the first fleet-capable LANTIRN pod was delivered to VF-103 at NAS Oceana. During the ceremony held to mark this occasion, Secretary of the Navy John H Dalton proudly proclaimed that 'The Cat is Back'.

To give an unsophisticated bomber like the F-14 a precision targeting capability, the basic LANTIRN system was modified into the US Navy-specific LTS (LANTIRN Targeting System) configuration. The LTS removed the navigation pod of the two-pod LANTIRN system and vastly improved the targeting pod for Tomcat use. The latter featured its own embedded global positioning system (GPS) and Inertial Measurement Unit (IMU) that provided the pod with line-of-sight cueing and weapon release ballistics.

Unlike the twin pod LANTIRN system used by the USAF, the LTS performed all the weapon release calculations automatically and then presented the release cues that it had generated via the cockpit displays in the F-14. It also incorporated a masking avoidance curve display and, eventually, a north orientation cue and a 40,000 ft-capable laser receiver. Only the F-14Ds of VF-213 and the F-14Bs of VF-102 had the upgrade altitude laser in the early stages of OEF, VF-14, VF-41 and VF-211 having to soldier on with the original LTS pods, which had a laser fire limiter set at 25,000 ft. The 40,000 ft pod quickly proved its worth in OEF by allowing F-14 aircrew to employ LGBs above potential threat system altitudes in the higher terrain of Afghanistan.

As a pseudo-reconnaissance asset, the LTS also generated coordinates for any target located via the pod's FLIR (Forward-Looking Infra-Red). A later software modification known as T3 (Tomcat Tactical Targeting) increased the accuracy of the coordinates produced by the LTS, and

A photographer's mate from VF-41 adjusts the aperture on the lens of a KS-153B long-range camera. Of the three sensors fitted in the TARPS pod, the KS-153B was usually the most important. Following the pod upgrade in the early 1990s, the KS-153B was interchangeable with the older KA-99 low altitude pan camera (*US Navy*)

Despite being a substantial 17 ft long, the TARPS pod still fitted snugly in the tunnel between the Tomcat's twin engines (*US Navy*)

allowed for the first rudimentary TACAIR onboard generation of coordinates suitable for JDAM, JSOW, the CBU-103 Wind-Corrected Munitions Dispenser and other coordinate-dependant GPS-guided weapon employment.

As previously mentioned, the Tomcat had had the chance to show what it was capable of both in Iraq and the Balkans, and now it was preparing for war again.

CVW-8 GETS READY

The first carrier to arrive on station off the coast of Pakistan, *Enterprise* spent more than three weeks sailing in large circles as CENTCOM planned for OEF. With so little known about potential targets in Afghanistan, both VF-14 and VF-41 had their work cut out for them when it came to strike planning. VF-41 CO Cdr Brian Gawne explained the task facing the 'Black Aces' in the lead up to OEF;

'Afghanistan was an immature theatre, so when it came to strike planning, we were starting from scratch. Just weeks earlier we had been performing strikes into southern Iraq, and when preparing for such missions we could reference charts, planning tools and strike imagery, as well as rely on the experience of senior naval aviators who had been flying OSW sorties for almost a decade. The value of crews studying digitised imagery of the target area had been reinforced during operations over Kosovo in 1999, and that is exactly what we had done during OSW. We did not have sufficient imagery for such study prior to OEF, however.'

Like CVW-8, the CAOC was desperate for up-to-date photographs of potential targets such as airfields, SAM and AAA sites, army barracks and terrorist training camps, and it authorised both VF-41 and VF-213 to fly a series of TARPS missions over Afghanistan starting in late September – VF-14 had no TARPS capability. One of the pilots to provide the fighter escort for several of these missions was VF-41's Lt Marcus Lopez;

'My first sorties over the beach were flown about a week prior to OEF kicking off, when we provided cover for TARPS jets flying reconnaissance runs over key targets in south-eastern Afghanistan. We were not opposed on these flights, entering enemy airspace "high and fast". These sorties also allowed us to plan where we needed the tanker tracks to be established once hostilities commenced. We also used the

flights to gather ELINT (electronic intelligence) data on enemy SAMs and radar-guided AAA – a Prowler flew with us throughout these missions, monitoring the Afghan response to our incursions into their airspace.'

Due to the extreme distances involved in these flights, VF-41 could not venture beyond Kandahar, in south-eastern Afghanistan, at this time because of the limited nature of the tanker support then in-theatre. Indeed, CVW-8's VS-31 was the only unit capable of providing aerial refuelling assets for the air wing during

these early reconnaissance runs, Vikings dragging the Tomcats and Prowlers as close to Afghanistan as they could manage, then briefly holding on the Pakistani side of the border while the TACAIR jets topped off their tanks, before returning to CVN-65.

By the time the reconnaissance package had headed out of Afghan airspace at the end of its TARPS run, replacement tankers had arrived on station to provide the jets with sufficient fuel to make it back to the ship. VS-31's support was critical, as the F-14 used a lot of fuel conducting a TARPS mission – VS-29 performed identical missions for VF-213's TARPS flights pre-OEF.

With their pre-OEF CAP mission over, Lt Cdr Van Kizer and his RIO Lt Dave Bailey keep their hands in the air, and away from the weapons activation panel, while armourers pin the pylon firing mechanisms for the ordnance attached to 'Tophatter 200'. A 40-mission veteran of Operation *Allied Force*, Lt Cdr Kizer would fly a further 20 sorties in OEF (*VF-14*)

'Fast Eagle 105' (BuNo 161615) keeps station off the right wing of a KC-10A while its charge – an RC-135V of the 55th Wing – tops off its tanks midway through an ELINT mission along the Afghan-Pakistan border on the eve of OEF (*VF-41*)

VF-41 RIO Lt John Kelly was also heavily involved in CVW-8's intelligence gathering push pre-OEF;

'We sometimes flew two or three TARPS missions a day during this period, and during those flights in which I participated, I got the feeling that virtually no one in Afghanistan knew that I was overflying the country at 20,000 ft. There was no threat, and our RHAW (Radar Homing And Warning) gear detected the odd random search radar hit here and there. We had no idea what we were taking photos of, simply using the big KS-153B long-range camera to get stills of various "lat/longs" that we had been instructed to overfly.

'These were classic Tomcat TARPS missions in respect to the fact that the admiral and the CAG staffers needed to get hot prints on deck for use by our own intel folks, as well as target analysts in the CAOC. In order to

satisfy this demand, VF-41 would have photographer's mates pulling the film canisters out of the TARPS pod while the jet was still winding down on the flightdeck. The negatives would then be hastily developed and prints run off and dispersed. Those going beyond the ship to the CAOC would have to be digitised for transmitting. We also manned CAPs (Combat Air Patrols) for USAF RC-135V/W 'Rivet Joint' and US Navy EP-3E ELINT/SIGINT (Electronic/Signals intelligence) platforms immediately prior to OEF commencing.'

Aside from the TARPS sorties that actually overflew southern Afghanistan, both air wings also performed several mirror-image strike missions from the Northern Arabian Sea up to the Afghan-Pakistan border during the first week of October. These sorties, involving divisions of Tomcats and Hornets carrying representative bomb loads, as well as Prowlers, Vikings and Hawkeyes in support, were flown along the newly-established 'driveways' through Pakistan that both air wings would strictly adhere to once the war started. Similar missions of an identical duration were also flown over open water to the south of both carriers.

All three Tomcat units started performing round-the-clock CAP missions along the Afghan-Pakistan border from 3 October, as by that time the first big wing tankers had started venturing into the area from bases in the Middle East. Lt Cdr Van Kizer of VF-14 flew his first CAP just 24 hours after these sorties had commenced, and he made the following notes about the mission in his diary after returning to CVN-65;

'Launched in aircraft "204" and logged a 6.5-hour flight, which ended with my 200th career day trap. Once airborne off the cat, we proceeded overhead "Mom" at 19,000 ft to get 3000 lbs of fuel from the S-3. Once tanking was complete, we headed up to PARET – the point marking the Pakistani coast – and then to the tanker track about 50 miles south of the Afghan border, where we met "Whistler 11", our KC-10 tanker. Got another 3000 lbs of fuel from him and then proceeded to a point 15 miles south of the Afghan border, where we capped for the next five hours.

'We stayed on CAP until we had just 8000 lbs of fuel left, and then proceeded back to the tanker track, where we got another 12,000 lbs of gas from tanker "Monarch 05", before heading back to our CAP station.

'Had a little excitement while manning this station when we heard that MiG-21s were airborne in Afghanistan. We got vectored onto them, with our closest point of approach being 100 miles, before "Bossman" – the airborne USAF AWACS – directed us to drop them and not to go any further north, as we had approached to within ten nautical miles of the Afghan border. The MiG-21s didn't come any further south and we were not going to get permission to cross the border unless they showed some kind of hostile intent/act. We stayed on station there for another 45 minutes until our vul time ended and two F-14Ds from VF-213 checked in and relieved us on station.

'Went back to "Monarch 06" and took on board another 10,000 lbs of fuel, before joining up as a four-aeroplane division with "Pappy" and "Odie" from VFA-15 and heading back to "Mom".

'Not five minutes after we went feet wet, and around 110 miles from the ship, I started to get a fluctuating hydraulic pressure light. Well I knew exactly what that meant, and at any time I could expect to lose my combined side hydraulics and would have to emergency blow the landing gear down. Well, to cut a long story short, that's what happened, and I managed to bring her back for an OK 4 wire pass after the longest flight, and most butt pain, I have ever had in a F-14A Tomcat.'

By now CVW-8 had been operating as the night carrier for about a week, the *Enterprise* battle group commander, Rear Admiral Henry Ulrich, having told CENTAF that his air wing was more than happy to perform the midnight-to-noon slot. His opposite number in the *Carl Vinson* battle group, Rear Admiral Thomas Zelibor, who was also the overall commander of Fifth Fleet's Task Force 50 in the Northern Arabian Sea, readily accepted. CVW-8 made the gradual switch to night operations two weeks prior to OEF commencing.

When performing the midnight-to-noon shift, CVW-8 would launch its first wave of aircraft between 2300 hrs and 2330 hrs. Typically remaining aloft for six hours, they would land back aboard the ship in total darkness. The second wave launched at 0200 hrs and returned just after dawn, while the third and final wave left the ship at 0400 hrs and recovered shortly before noon.

On 4 October, with OEF mission planning now all but complete, the CAOC instructed the air wing commanders to brief their squadron COs on the opening phase of the campaign. VF-14 boss Cdr Bruce Fecht was present at the meeting aboard the 'Big E';

'CAG Mercer called the COs together in his office to provide direction on the upcoming campaign. It was only then that we knew OEF was likely to go ahead. It was time to get specific strike package assignments, targets and plans together. Initially, it was decided that VF-213 would cover the northern, high-altitude targets with their Tomcats due to the fact that they had the increased capability 40,000 ft LTS pods. As it turned out, however, CVW-8 was also assigned three high-altitude targets, which were to be hit in the second wave of strikes – an effort towards Kandahar, a second effort to the southwest against known terrorist camps, and a third effort, which I was part of, towards Kabul.'

As Cdr Fecht explained, CVW-11's F-14Ds would lead the first carrier-based strike of OEF, with VF-213's Cdr Chip King being mission commander. The D-model Tomcat was a formidable strike aircraft, as Cdr King related to the Author;

'Given the distance involved and the type of mission to be flown on the first night of OEF, there was no more capable a platform in the Navy, Air Force or Marine Corps than the F-14D. The Tomcat had two sets of eyes, long legs, superior communications and situational awareness through its Link 16 JTIDS (Joint Tactical Information Distribution System – only installed in the D-model), the ability to prosecute the target using the LTS pod and, more importantly, the ability to capture target imagery before and after the attack and transmit it back to CVN-70 in real time.'

Having spent almost four weeks sailing in circles in the Northern Arabian Sea while airspace clearance through Pakistan was secured, CSAR, tanker and AWACS assets organised themselves in-theatre and the MAAP was formulated and agreed upon within CENTCOM, the start of OEF could not come soon enough for VF-14, VF-41 and VF-213. On 7 October 2001, the naval aviators of these units, supported by myriad sailors aboard CVN-65 and CVN-70, prepared to play their part in the US-led fight back in the Global War on Terror.

OEF BEGINS

Operation *Enduring Freedom* commenced on the evening of Sunday, 7 October 2001, when, according to USAF Gen Richard Myers, Chairman of the Joint Chiefs of Staff, 'about 15 land-based bombers, some 25 strike aircraft from carriers and US and British ships and submarines, launching approximately 50 Tomahawk missiles, have struck terrorist targets in Afghanistan'.

Although the F-14s, F/A-18s and EA-6Bs of CVW-11 and, several hours later, CVW-8 would be in the vanguard of the action, the first aircraft sortied were actually USAF types despatched from bases in the American Midwest. B-2s, along with five B-1Bs and ten B-52Hs flying from the US Navy Support Facility on Diego Garcia (an atoll in the Indian Ocean), hit Taleban early warning radar sites and other air defence related targets, as dictated by the CAOC's Master Air Attack Plan.

Commenting on the targets chosen during a Department of Defense press briefing held on the opening day of OEF, Donald Rumsfeld said that the first priority of the campaign was to 'remove the threat from air defences and from Taleban aircraft. We need the freedom to operate on the ground and in the air, and the targets selected, if successfully destroyed, should permit an increasing degree of freedom over time'.

Charged with both hitting targets and providing protection for the USAF heavy bombers whilst over Afghanistan, VF-213's F-14Ds would go into combat on that first night of OEF in true strike-fighter configuration. The unit's 'gunner' was ordnanceman CWO3 Michael Lavoie, and it was his job to oversee the arming of the four Tomcats that led CVW-11's opening OEF strike. Despite having worked carrier flightdecks for 20+ years, Lavoie had never seen such heavily laden F-14s launched from a carrier prior to the evening of 7 October 2001;

'On the first night of OEF, our aircraft were hitting pre-planned targets, so we knew what ordnance was required. We had four jets heading out, and we uploaded bombs in quantities that we had never previously hung on a VF-213 aircraft – two of the Tomcats carried pairs of 1000-lb GBU-16s, and the remaining jets were armed with 500-lb GBU-12s. We also armed each of them with single AIM-54C Phoenix and AIM-7M Sparrow missiles, as well as two AIM-9L Sidewinders and 678 rounds for their 20 mm cannon. The jets were prepared for anything, as we had little idea about what kind of air threat would be opposing us.

'I truly wondered whether these aircraft were going to get off the

The crew of VF-213's 'Blacklion 103' (BuNo 163899) prepare to launch from CVN-70's waist catapult on the opening night of OEF. The unit would spearhead CTF-50's strikes on Kabul and Herat, with a section of F-14Ds being sent to attack targets in both cities. VF-213 had six '40/K' LTS pods for its aircraft, and these proved vital right from the word go in OEF. This particular jet was paired up with pod 22, which was responsible for lasing 59 LGBs during the unit's time in-theatre. Some 44 of these bombs achieved near or direct hits on their designated targets (*Lt Andrew Mickley*)

Lt Cdr Michael Peterson (left) and Cdr Chip King participated in VF-213's Kabul strike on the opening night of OEF, and also routinely flew together throughout the campaign. Both men were seasoned naval aviators by the time they saw combat over Afghanistan, with Cdr King being CVW-11's senior strike lead and Lt Cdr Peterson having seen combat as a Strike Weapons and Tactics Instructor augmentee with VF-14 and VF-41 in Operation *Allied Force*. One of the first FAC(A)-qualified Tomcat RIOs, Lt Cdr Peterson would also participate in OIF – with VF-2 – in 2003. Their jet is armed with two GBU-12s, the 500-lb LGB being VF-213's staple weapon – 271 dropped – in OEF (*Cdr Michael Peterson*)

deck laden down with all this weaponry. We had spent the previous weeks before going to war precisely weighing all the ordnance that might be hung from a Tomcat in OEF, and then calculating what the aircraft could carry. We had a programme devised on our computers that would allow us to accurately calculate the weight of the various weapons configurations. We ran through literally hundreds of potential mission loads, and in turn gave the weights to the CO and CAG so that they could devise their strike plans. Weight is a critical thing for carrier-based jets, as the catapult has to be correctly adjusted to provide adequate thrust to ensure that the aircraft will fly after being launched.

'I watched with anxious fascination as we launched jets armed with two GBU-16s, four missiles and all the gas that could be squeezed into them to the point where the aircraft weighed in at 72,000 lbs apiece.'

Strapped into 'Blacklion 101' on 7 October was VF-213 CO Cdr Chip King, who had been selected by his CAG, Capt Thomas C Bennett, to lead the CVW-11 strike;

'CAG chose me to head up this mission because I was the senior strike lead in CVW-11 at the time, and the F-14D was the premier precision bombing platform in the air wing. Unlike other Tomcats in-theatre, our jets had all the "toys", with Link-16 JTIDS (Joint Tactical Information Distribution System) being the most important. This system allowed us to use the datalink to deconflict with all other assets in our package without having to use our radio or radar, as well as letting us quickly find the tanker when gas got critical. And with my LTS pod featuring the new "40K" laser, we could drop our LGBs from heights up to 40,000 ft MSL – well outside of the Taleban AAA/SAM threat envelope.

'The plan for the opening strikes of OEF called for a multi-prong, nearly simultaneous attack by Tomcat-led packages on western and eastern military targets within Afghanistan, followed by the final arm – all Hornets – striking the airfield at Kandahar. The lead element, consisting of two F-14Ds in the swing strike/fighter roles, two F/A-18Cs, an EA-6B and two B-1Bs, would attack the target in the east – an SA-3 "Goa" missile site and support facility near Kabul's international airport.

'We briefed the overall strike coordination aboard CVN-70 during the afternoon of 7 October, with all the senior leadership in attendance. My element had two missions to perform. The first was to "sweep" the airspace in front of an element of B-1Bs to clear it of any enemy fighters that were foolish enough to launch against our strike package. Afghan air force MiG-21s reportedly almost never flew at night, but we nevertheless hoped that they would launch and give us a chance for an air-to-air kill.

'Our second mission was to deliver additional ordnance on the SA-3 site, which was due to be hit by TLAMs minutes prior to our arrival.

The LGBs that we dropped would ensure that the SAM battery, and its "Spoon Rest" and "Low Blow" target acquisition and guidance radars, remained out of commission for future strikes on Kabul. The Hornets were to launch and guide a single AGM-84 SLAM-ER (Stand-off Land Attack Missile - Expanded Response) from a significant distance away from the target to impact in the same area, while the EA-6B provided radar jamming support to mask our approach and departure.

'Following the overall brief, we broke down into individual element briefs, which concluded approximately two hours prior to the planned launch. Rear Admiral Tom Zelibor reminded us that we still did not have an execute order, so as we began to ascend to the flightdeck at 1740 hrs, we still did not know if the mission was a go or not.

'It was at this point that I remember seeing numerous flashes on the horizon all around us, and within moments there was a hush as everyone was transfixed by this activity. We all seemed to have come to the realisation of what those flashes were at the same time – the "small boys" (cruisers and destroyers) and submarines were launching TLAMs. The Tomahawks provided the opening salvos in the Global War on Terror.

'As the missiles climbed into the dusk sky, a loud cheer resonated across the flightdeck, which was followed almost immediately by an eerie calm as the Air Boss called away to start our engines and prepare to launch! The launch progressed flawlessly and our strike package rendezvous and transit to the tanker was also uneventful.

'An E-2C crew from CVW-11's VAW-117 performed excellent coordination while we transited north through Pakistani airspace, and we conducted a package roll call on the way to our front side tanker. On the first night of the war, there were no AWACS or tanker assets located over Afghanistan. The corridor of airspace negotiated for Coalition use with Pakistan had an east and west boundary that required us to meet a drogue-configured KC-135, receive our allotted gas and then fly a 500-nautical-mile round trip to Kabul and back to the tanker assigned to our package. We would then get our backside gas, before returning to the carrier

'As we joined up on the KC-135 on night vision goggles, we could see that something was wrong. There was a solid stream of gas trailing from the "knuckle" where the drogue hose connected to the hard refuelling boom. While the fighters, given their probe placement to the right side of their windscreens, were still able to take gas, the EA-6B pilot could not tank without obstructing his vision because his probe was located almost directly in front of his windscreen. I decided that given the minimal threat – one SA-3 "Goa" SAM, AAA and shoulder-launched MANPADS (Man-Portable Air Defence System) – the EA-6B should return home.

'We were supposed to get about 8000 lbs of gas each, but the boom operator told us "off load complete" when we had barely received 3000 lbs due to the amount of gas streaming out of the leak.

'To make matters worse, this KC-135 was also supposed to be our backside tanker when we came out of country. However, because of the leak, it would not be available upon our return. I requested that the USAF AWACS controller who was now handling us coordinate and find my strike package a spare or alternate tanker – he would have approximately one hour to make these arrangements. We pressed on to Kabul, not knowing what our refuelling options would be off target.'

Manning the second jet in Cdr King's section were Lt John Saccomando and Lt Cdr Michael Peterson, and the latter recalled;

'We were able to maintain regular (UHF) communications with the AWACS in Pakistan for a while, but soon we only had contact using our JTIDS voice channels. Eventually we could only talk with the members of our package, having received a check-in from the B-1Bs confirming their position. At least the rules of engagement were easy for us to understand. If anyone launched in front of us, they weren't friendly and could be engaged after meeting a few other simple criteria.'

The weather was clear as the Tomcats and Hornets flew north up the Khyber Pass, with the moon breaking the horizon to the northeast of the strike aircraft. The Hornets, positioned outside the lead section of Tomcats, were to launch their solitary SLAM-ER when 50 nautical miles from their target – located near to the SA-3 site that the VF-213 jets were tasked with destroying – and guide it from a safe distance using a datalink pod on the wing aircraft. Lt Cdr Peterson explained to the Author that moments after the Hornets executed their turn outbound, the horizon again lit up as the TLAMs began raining down on their targets;

'Even though we were more than 100 nautical miles from the target when the Tomahawks impacted, you could see the flashes right on time through our NVGs. A few minutes after the impacts, something else was quite evident on the NVGs – the entire capital had erupted with AAA.

'The Taleban may not have had more than one radar-guided SAM guarding Kabul, but these guys had a shitload of AAA! It looked like you could get out of the jet and walk across it. I could see tracers from rapid-fire smaller-calibre guns (both 23 mm and 58 mm) burning out below us. They also had bigger weapons in the capital as well, with some of these guns having been moved up into the mountains that ringed the city – Kabul itself is located in excess of 6000 ft mean sea level (MSL), with surrounding mountains that reach 12,000+ ft in elevation. Shells from these weapons exploded at far higher altitudes, and from where we were sitting, they looked like an Independence Day fireworks show. You could see a faint sparkling trail from these single round heavy calibre shells as they penetrated the mass of smaller fires and sailed on up to our altitude, before exploding with a brilliant bang.

'Fortunately, the Navy had upgraded the laser in our LTS pods to allow it to fire at altitudes up to 40,000 ft MSL (instead of the old maximum altitude of 25,000 ft). Descending to 25,000 ft MSL to fire the laser for LGB guidance would have put us well into the heart of the AAA. Some of the bigger guns could still reach up and touch us at 40,000 ft, but the fires up there weren't nearly as dense as the concentration below us.'

With the mountains surrounding Kabul blocking the view of the city lights from the Tomcat crews until they had banked to the east around a range of peaks, Cdr King could not set up his attack run until the last minute. This meant that although they were flying the trailing F-14D, Lt Saccomando and Lt Cdr Peterson dropped the first bombs of OEF.

'As we turned to the east over the capital to line up for our attack run, we were able to maintain our altitude well above 30,000 ft MSL, but being up this high also had its drawbacks', recalled RIO Lt Cdr Peterson. 'The release range for our two GBU-12s was much farther away from the target, and that made it considerably harder to identify the SAM site

through the LTS. Nevertheless, we located our target and released on timeline. Then my NVGs lit up as I saw our lead engage afterburner and spin a quick 360-degree turn over the target area. They had located their target late and were inside release range, so they decided to re-attack.

'We guided our weapons on target, but they went slightly long. We later found out that they hit a barracks just beyond the intended point of impact. We flew out ahead of our lead towards Jalalabad and cleared the airspace for the B-1Bs, who were 20+ nautical miles in trail.'

In 'Blacklion 101', Cdr King and his RIO, Lt Cdr Paul Gronemeyer, were working hard to get their GBU-16s off on target;

'We made a hard right turn, continually doing belly checks, while trying to maintain our energy package – difficult to do when flying at 30,000 ft MSL. By the time we came out of the turn, we had lost nearly 8000 ft and 50 knots! We acquired the target and released our weapons, and I unloaded the jet so as to accelerate to 500 knots and begin a gentle climb back above 30,000 ft. We picked up our wingman, who was already heading south, on JTIDS, and it was then that we realised we were well behind our established timeline. Our wingman throttled back to save gas and allow us to close on him. Having re-established section integrity within ten minutes, the hunt for a tanker now commenced in earnest.'

By the time the two jets had joined up, Lt Cdr Peterson had already made several attempts at contacting their AWACS controller to determine the location of their backside tanker. The VF-213 jets had flown 100 nautical miles south from the target area by the time contact was made with their controller. Cdr King's first job was to confirm that a tanker was on station on the northeastern 'driveway' as planned.

However, according to Lt Cdr Peterson, 'the controller calmly told us that the leaky tanker had returned to base, and a new tanker had taken its place on another track. He then passed the tanker's call-sign and track location. We pulled out the chart and looked for the new tanker track, and to our horror found out that it was located not in the northeastern but central part of the Pakistani airspace, more than 400 nautical miles away! We immediately went to a maximum fuel conservation profile, climbing above 40,000 ft and slowing down significantly, even though we were still deep in enemy territory.

'Blacklion 101' (BuNo 164603) led the first manned strike of OEF, when Tomcats and Hornets from CVW-11 hit an SA-3 SAM battery, and its attendant target acquisition and guidance radars, near Kabul's international airport on 7 October 2001. The second to last Tomcat ever built, this aircraft was originally delivered to VF-124 on 29 May 1992 and subsequently became one of the first D-model aircraft assigned to VF-2 in June of the following year. Transferred to VF-213 in late 1997, the jet remained with the 'Black Lions' until passed on to VF-101 in early 2002. BuNo 164603 returned to the fleet in the summer of 2003 when the aircraft was sent to VF-31 and soon became its 'Felix 101' jet. Completing a further two cruises with the unit, the Tomcat had the distinction of making the very last flight by a Navy F-14 on 4 October 2006 when it flew from NAS Oceana to Republic Airport, in Farmingdale, New York. The aircraft presently resides in the American Airpower Museum at Farmingdale, but will eventually be put on display as a memorial to all Northrop Grumman workers at nearby Bethpage (*Lt Tony Toma*)

'We tried to get the tanker moved to the original station to meet us, but the AWACS said that he had other customers that needed him to remain on his current track. We ran the numbers and predicted that we would arrive on the tanker track with 3000 lbs of gas each. This was probably not enough fuel to get us to the emergency divert airfield at Jacobabad, in southern Pakistan, if there was a problem on the tanker.

'As we approached the tanker track in an idle power descent to save gas, we made contact with the KC-135 and explained the situation.

Congestion on the tanker was a common problem facing Tomcat crews returning from long-range strikes short on fuel. This photograph was taken during front side refuelling, however, when fuel was not so critical for F-14 crews. Getting on the tanker expeditiously was always an issue for pilots flying the notoriously short-legged Hornet. Here, a section of F/A-18Cs from VFA-94 take it in turns to top off their tanks from a Diego Garcia-based KC-10A assigned to the 32nd Aerial Refueling Squadron/305th Air Mobility Wing (*Lt Tony Toma*)

Surrounded by high peaks, Kabul proved to be a challenging target for Tomcats and Hornets throughout OEF. The SA-3 site attacked by CVW-11 on night one of the war was situated near the international airport seen at the extreme left in this photo (*Lt Cdr Jim Muse*)

He started dragging his receivers towards us, and had us call his turn so that we would wind up right behind him in position to refuel without wasting gas having to join up and get in position on our own. As we gained a visual on the tanker, with a division of four F/A-18 "chicks in tow", he cleared out the rest of the aircraft waiting to refuel and allowed us to join right on the boom. The KC-135 crew had performed flawlessly in getting us into the basket as expeditiously as possible.

'Our lead's fuel state was lower than ours, with "Blacklion 101" having only 3200 lbs of fuel left in its tanks, so Cdr King quickly plugged in. Having taken on just 2000 lbs of "comfort fuel", he then disengaged to the starboard side and allowed us to get all the gas that we required. As we plugged and the fuel began to flow, I noted that we had only 2000 lbs of gas left – not enough for us to have made it to the emergency divert. After getting a few thousand pounds, our lead cycled back through and we were able to head back to the ship for an uneventful recovery.'

GO WEST

While Cdr King led his strike package to Kabul, VF-213's executive officer, Cdr Anthony Giaini, and his wingman were tasked with protecting B-1Bs bombing the air base at Herat, before heading to Farah and attacking a Taleban communications facility with their own LGBs. Both targets were in western Afghanistan, not far from the country's border with Iran. The F-14 was the only carrier-based jet that could perform a mission such as this, as Cdr Giaini explained;

'The strike I led on the first night of the war reflected both the realities imposed on us by the limited number of assets we could support (particularly with tankers), the ranges

involved and the kind of enemy we faced. Unless, and until, we could eliminate the air defences in Afghanistan, the tankers would not be going in-country. The result was that the Tomcats hit the far targets in Kabul and Herat and the Hornets hit the nearer ones in and around Kandahar.

'In reality, all three locations were a real stretch, requiring precise planning, absolute discipline and jets kept in top shape. We were blessed to have all three. In fact, I would go so far as to say that range and endurance were as much a weapon as the LGBs we carried – without the Tomcat's ability to reach distant targets and return to the tankers unrefuelled, the campaign might have lasted much longer. And I believe it is safe to say that other missions – particularly SCAR (Strike Coordination of Armed Reconnaissance) and CAS (Close-Air Support) – would have had a significantly different flavour without the F-14's qualities.'

Having refuelled from an S-3 and a KC-135 en route to Afghanistan, Cdr Giaini and his pilot, Lt Cdr Kevin Claffy, led their wingman to the rendezvous point, where they joined up right on time with a division of Diego Garcia-based B-1B strikers for the Herat attack.

'The plan was for us to take on several missions during the course of the evening', Cdr Giaini recalled. 'Meet up with the B-1 "Bones", push well ahead of them on a sweep mission and thus prevent any MiGs which might get airborne from disrupting the runway bombing at Herat. Aside from engaging and destroying any enemy fighters that succeeded in taking off, we had also been tasked with striking the Taleban communications facility at Farah, time and fuel permitting,

'As we crossed the border, I made the secure call "Indian country", and we reconfigured our jet to make ourselves invisible without the aid of NVGs. The result was amazing – a dark country full of small towns, few lights, less the impact of TLAMs and the angry dome of AAA created by Taleban gunners in response, intent on shooting something down.

'Requests to the AWACS for a "picture" – a description of what their long-range radar was showing – became less frequent as the miles marched on. After a while, they too were out of range. It was now down to the "Bones" and the "Toms". We said very little, growing in confidence that we would not be intercepted as we flew deeper and deeper into Afghanistan. Once the B-1s had attacked Herat, they would exit the theatre into safe territory, and they would no longer be our responsibility.

'With our radar showing no airborne contacts, I slewed the FLIR onto the airfield and was surprised to see a pristine MiG-21 sitting on the ramp, attached to a start cart and huffer! It was obvious that this jet was being held on Quick-Reaction Alert, but clearly no one had notified the base of our approach. I slewed the FLIR onto the target and punched the laser for a range update – seconds to go. Lt Cdr Claffy and I decided that if this guy took off we'd kill him. If not, then we'd take him with an LGB.

'As the miles marched down, it became apparent that there was no activity around this jet. Why was the MiG-21 seemingly deserted? Was the pilot on strip alert, waiting for someone to tell him to take off? Could it be that the airfield, like us, was out of comms range, or perhaps the base's radars and radios were being blocked by our jammers or had been knocked out by our TLAM attacks on their communications nodes?

'In a matter of moments we reached the release point, and I held my breath as though I were shooting a rifle, conscious of the fact that I had never before delivered an LGB – never mind one in combat. I watched the white hot GBU-12 streak toward the target on my FLIR picture, hitting the MiG-21 amidships and blowing chunks of the aircraft all over the airfield. "Good kill, good kill", my pilot and I whispered to each other as I punched the radar back into air-to-air mode.

'A few minutes later, a column of explosions began to appear along the runway – evidence that the "Bones" had done their job, and they then disappeared to the north, happy, I'm sure, to be leaving Afghanistan behind them. We, on the other hand, had a long way to go just to reach the security of the next tanker in Pakistan. Lt Cdr Claffy, being an experienced pilot, had already begun to sweat this problem – we climbed to our maximum range profile and pushed south.

'We were far out of range of the AWACS, or any other American, for that matter. As the mission commander and strike lead, I decided that since we had successfully completed the first two missions (getting the "Bones" though to Herat and neutralising any threats that potentially stood in their path), we would have just enough fuel to complete the third assignment of our strike – destroy the comms facility at Farah. So we headed south along the Afghan-Iran border, and after a short time we spotted the lights of Farah on the FLIR.

'Unlike other cities, lit by the impact of weapons and illuminated by AAA, Farah seemed strangely quiet, with its streets deserted. The target area – a group of rather small buildings within a walled compound – looked different from the limited imagery that we had been provided with. In fact, it was a bit ambiguous. As the target set was in the middle of a fairly sizeable city, it was absolutely crucial that we got this right – we couldn't bomb targets in the middle of a city and hope for the best. As a result of this uncertainty, I made the decision to overfly the target to ensure positive identification of the buildings.

'I also wanted to deliver our weapons in such a fashion that the frag (blast pattern) would stay in the compound, and that any long bombs – when the LGB's tail fins fail to open, the weapon will usually impact beyond the target – would also land in the compound too. This extra overflight burned precious fuel that we didn't really have available. Fortunately for us, we managed to strike our targets in two simultaneous hits on the next pass, destroying the buildings and, I am proud to say, without the frag "splash" escaping the compound.'

Like Cdr King's section, Cdr Giaini and his wingman were now faced with a fuel crunch following the successful completion of all three of their missions. Turning south in search of a tanker track, both F-14Ds were well below their planned fuel state. However, once they had managed to raise their AWACS controller via JTIDS, their call for an available tanker was met by an immediate response from 'Bossman' (the AWACS controller's most frequently used call-sign), and off they went to meet it.

Once they found the KC-135, Cdr Giaini was dismayed to discover that he and his wingman were numbers five and six in the queue for fuel behind a division of Hornets from CVW-8 that were en route to their target. To make matters worse, they were unable to communicate with the F/A-18s for some reason, although they could speak to the tanker.

'After our fuel dipped to 2500 lbs – we were only just south of the Afghan-Pakistan border – I managed to convince the Hornets and tanker

to let us to the front of the queue', Cdr Giaini explained.

'My wingman and I were very happy to get a few thousand pounds just to keep us going, before heading back to the end of the line. Eventually, we topped off and flew back to the carrier. We landed nearly eight hours after we had taken off, and when we shut down, we found that the maintenance personnel who had launched us – and many who hadn't – had stayed up all night to make sure that we made it back aboard.'

Armed with a pair of 1000-lb GBU-16 LGBs, 'Blacklion 101' closes on a KC-10 for front side gas during an early OEF mission. VF-213 expended 157 GBU-16s during the campaign, primarily against fixed targets. Bomb loadouts were constantly altered as the war progressed, and VF-213's air-to-ground weapons training officer, Lt John Saccomando, detailed some of these changes in a report he submitted to Commander, Fighter Wing US Atlantic Fleet post-cruise;

'OEF proved to be challenging for VF-213 with respect to aircraft configuration, authorised loadouts, high angle visual delivery techniques and unexpended ordnance bring-back options. With an ever-changing load plan in the Air Tasking Order, it was very challenging to maximise our ordnance flexibility on station, while being prepared to bring it all back. CVW-11 mandated a 2800-lb minimum fuel "on the ball" in the daytime and 3800-lb at night. With our average F-14D weighing in at around 48,000 lbs with weapons rails, we were forced to designate our four lightest aircraft as "quad bombers". For the daytime, this proved very effective with a war load of four GBU-12s. At night, however, even the lightest jet could only recover with three GBU-12s.

'In the early stages of the war, the ATO called for two Mk 83s and two GBU-16s for some of the CAS missions. Because this loadout is not recoverable, standard operating procedure was to jettison the "dumb bombs" if they were not dropped in Afghanistan' (USAF)

CVW-8 ENTERS THE FRAY

As the night carrier, *Enterprise* had to wait until the early hours of 8 October before its strike aircraft could bomb their targets. Like CVW-11, CVW-8 would send two F-14As from VF-14 to strike the 'Spoon Rest' A-band warning and target acquisition radar that provided guidance for the SA-3 SAM battery at Kabul. The latter had, of course, been struck earlier that night by TLAMs and two Tomcats from VF-213. Elsewhere, a pair of F-14As from VF-41 would target the cave entrance to an al-Qaeda training camp in mountains near Kandahar.

While the Tomcat crews involved in these attacks underwent their final pre-mission briefs, air wing staff officer Lt Cdr Bill Lind was monitoring the campaign's early progress in CVN-65's CVIC;

'I spent 7/8 October standing the watch for CVW-8's Strike Warfare Commander, which we stood in CVIC to ensure good connectivity and rapid flexibility when the tasking from above, or the tactical situation, changed. The watch I stood had radio, e-mail and chat connectivity with the CAOC in Saudi Arabia. This was the nexus from which the war was run, and from which we got our tasking, and it also provided me with an opportunity to see how things were done in OEF.

'The complexion of the war was changing minute by minute even in that early stage. All our strikes that night had pre-assigned targets and loadouts. However, as new intelligence came to light and the results from *Carl Vinson*'s strikes filtered in, many of our missions changed. Our ordnance personnel, led by Lt Cdr Ed Haislip, did amazing work rearming jets at the last minute as tasking dictated.

'CVW-8 had spent a lot of time in work-ups perfecting the skills required to perform Time-Sensitive Strikes (TSTs). A fairly new concept at the time, TST entailed the ability to rapidly alter tasking and strike emerging (usually mobile) targets with little or no prior planning. Although simple in theory, the preparation and command and control to ensure that everyone was on the same page could be tricky. The key was staying inside the enemy's decision loop, in that we would find, analyse and strike a target before he had the wherewithal to move or conceal it. Our training, from the intel personnel in CVIC analysing and preparing target data, to the ordnancemen swapping bombs, to aircrew junking hours of pre-flight planning to flex to new targets, paid off handsomely.

'The first night for CVW-8 was highlighted by almost 100 per cent good effects on every target we hit. Our Hornets flew almost exclusively with GPS-guided Joint Direct Attack Munitions (JDAM), striking cave complexes and other command and control nodes. The Tomcats did great work along the same lines, including two sorties carrying large GBU-24 penetrating LGBs, hitting some very deep caves which were almost impossible to find via the jets' LTS FLIR.'

CVW-8's attack on the Kabul SA-3 radar site was to be spearheaded by a pair of F-14As from VF-14, with squadron CO, Cdr Bruce Fecht, acting as the strike lead;

'Initially, a section of Hornets, a section of Tomcats and some support assets, including a Prowler, were fragged to carry out this mission. As detailed planning got underway in the lead up to A-Day, it became clear that there would be insufficient fuel available for the F/A-18s to make it from the last tanker to the target area. The strike package quickly degraded to just two Tomcats from VF-14 and a Prowler from VAQ-141 – not exactly the force we would have planned to put up for a first night strike had we been conducting an air wing training evolution from Fallon!

'The instructors at the Naval Strike and Air Warfare Center would have castigated us for being so cavalier and nonconformist in our tactics and plans. However, logistics and operational necessity dictated that this would indeed be the first strike package from CVN-65 in OEF.'

Other elements that were not optimal affected the planning and execution of that particular mission. The high altitude of the targets and the ceiling-restricted performance of the old LTS pods fitted to VF-14's jets shaped the bomb delivery plan devised by Cdr Fecht and his operations department. Identified by veteran Tomcat RIOs as the 'weakest link' in the original AN/AAQ-25 LTS pod as delivered to the Navy, the laser receiver (not the transmitter) had the potential to 'arc and spark' above 25,000 ft MSL. This fault could cause a fire in the pod, and with the LTS being non-jettisonable, that eventually meant an aircraft

Four GBU-16s and a GBU-12, destined to be dropped by VF-41 on the first night of OEF, are seen with their fireproof ablative coatings covered in graffiti applied by 'ordies' in the ship's armoury. The unit dropped 103 GBU-16s and 92 GBU-12s (as well as five GBU-10s and two GBU-24s) in just 16 days. 'Our ordnance gave us few problems in OEF', recalled Lt Cdr David Lobdell of VF-41. 'In 1999, when conducting my pre-flight checks prior to flying bombing missions over Kosovo, I routinely saw LGBs date stamped "manufactured in 1972" that had been uploaded onto my jet. Despite being some 20 years past their warranty date, for the most part they hit nicely. By OEF, we had newer weapons that were still under warranty, and we had no problems with them' (*Cdr Brian Gawne*)

An EA-6B Prowler accompanied most of the strike packages sent into Afghanistan in the early days of the campaign (*Lt Tony Toma*)

fire too. Once this problem was discovered, a software restriction was placed into the pod that inhibited laser fire above 25,000 ft MSL.

With the new '40K' laser-modified pods, which reached the fleet in early 2001, Lockheed Martin replaced the old laser receiver (and a few other pieces of internal hardware) with an improved, more powerful one, and also modified and upgraded the software to allow laser system functionality up to 40,000 ft MSL. Old pods were progressively reworked to this standard, and a number of new ones procured.

Only VF-213 and VF-102 had received the '40K' pods by the time OEF commenced, thus severely restricting the attack profiles that VF-14 and VF-41 could fly when attacking fixed targets in cities such as Kabul. As previously noted, the Afghan capital is situated at 6000 ft+ MSL and surrounded by mountains with peaks in excess of 12,000 ft MSL.

'The performance of our LTS pods, the close proximity of the target impact points, considerations about the timing of our attack runs due to possible smoke/dust clouds over the target and defensive measures to counter SAMs and AAA drove the route tactics that we adopted', explained Cdr Fecht. 'In effect, we determined that it was best for Pk (probability of kill) to violate another basic tenet in strike planning and opt for a re-attack along a similar (but reciprocal) heading to allow for the second target to be hit with the needed lethality. When you examined the plan overall, it looked pretty shaky – a first night attack on a "centre-of-gravity" Taleban target, with limited altitude sanctuary, a minimal strike package and a planned re-attack on the initial (but reciprocal) heading. I don't think many folks would sign up to this in training.'

Having launched, the small CVW-8 strike package headed north and reached Pakistan without any drama. However, shortly after going 'feet dry', Cdr Fecht's 'Dash-2' jet, piloted by Lt Cdr Marcell Padilla (and with Lt Cdr Art delaCruz as his RIO), reported smoke in the cockpit. 'We had a power spike that caused the loss of our INS (Inertial Navigation System) and saw the cockpit fill with smoke and fumes', recalled Lt Cdr Padilla.

'I told "Cutlass 43" (Cdr Fecht) that I had seen "arcs and sparks" and had shut down the Weapon Control System in order to avoid the possibility of a fire. After careful consideration, the system was brought back online and my RIO and I assessed our ability to continue the mission. It appeared that the AWG-15 (stores management system) and LTS were unaffected, so we chose to press on without an operable radar.'

Happy that his wingman could still fly the mission, Cdr Fecht now prepared himself for aerial refuelling;

'The next big hurdle was tanking. Lights out, higher altitude than normal and with little room for error, this was a critical node for the sortie. The use of the FLIR pod and NVGs eased the concerns surrounding the lights out rendezvous with the tanker. Nevertheless, whenever we worked with the KC-135 "Iron Maiden" (a nickname derived from the 16th century torture device that naval aviators felt perfectly summed up their experiences refuelling from the probe and rigid drogue-equipped boom of the veteran Boeing tanker), we expected to use lots of concentration just to stay in the basket.

'The way we were configured, and at the altitude (30,000 ft) the tanker was flying at in order to remain out of any SAM envelopes, we were having to use a little afterburner on one engine to stay in the basket after reaching about 16,000 lbs of fuel onboard. My technique was a little tap of afterburner – around Zone 2 – on the port engine and then use the right engine to modulate any further power needs. This worked for me, and it was a big relief to meet the tanker and complete that part of the mission, knowing that we now had enough fuel to get to the target and make the divert airfield if there was no tanker available on the backside.

'After all three aircraft had cleared the tanker, it wasn't long before we crossed the border and were eerily on our way up the valley from Kandahar to Kabul. The city was dark and seemingly quiet. It wasn't like that on the computer simulation that I had trained on in the days leading up to this moment, and not what I had expected. We knew that the TLAMs had hit their targets in the area, and I assumed they had taken down the electrical grid. This lack of lighting had no effect whatsoever on the LTS, however, which soon started to break out the target so that it resembled the intel photographs that we had pored over pre-mission.

'After my RIO and I had verified the target, we got ready to drop our GBU-16s. My next step was to lift the arming guard and set the switch to "ARM" – something I had done numerous times in training, but this was the first time I had ever done it "in anger". I "pickled" the bombs and felt the "thunk" of the release as they fell away. We then made a 2-3G left turn to set ourselves up for the lasing portion of the drop.

'After attaining the angles I wanted, we turned to the right and concentrated on the final portion of the strike – guiding the weapon through the laser spot via the RIO's weapon station. During this part of the mission I was the only one looking out of the cockpit, since the RIOs in both jets were concentrating on the sensor displays and backing each other up on the delivery tactics. My wing pilot was busy formation flying, trying to stay in position. Therefore, when the bombs hit the target, I was the only one to initially see the returning ground fire.

'"Hey, look at that, they're shooting at us. Low, right, five o'clock". I saw the tracers firing from the dark world below. Although they were heading in our general direction, I felt confident that they were behind us and not aimed with the proper lead needed.

'As we headed north, we saw the airport to the northeast of us start to light up with ground fire. It appeared that the gunners had a bead on us, but it was hard to tell if they were just following the noise or actually had a sensor on us. There were at least six different centres of fire I could determine, and we had been briefed that the airport would be heavily fortified. However, we had to fly around it clockwise from the southwest to the southeast so as to line up for our wingman's bombing run.

'As we started to make our turn back to the south, we knew we were bleeding knots too quickly, and that we would require afterburner to restore our airspeed – this would highlight us in the night sky. We didn't want to help the Taleban improve their targeting solution, but we had a certain minimum airspeed we had to maintain for manoeuvrability and threat avoidance. Somewhere in that turn I also passed the lead to my wingman and then tried to hold on for the ride.

'About the time we were getting onto a southerly heading, I was now flying sucked and left of the lead, looking around for the greatest threat. There was plenty of stuff flying through the air, with lots of bullets and an occasional missile being sighted. In fact the view in my NVGs got so

concentrated with glowing green dots that I decided it was time to take them off and just follow the afterburner of the lead. I could see bullets to the right of us and bullets to the left of us, and I was praying that they were going to miss and fall down on each other. It was better with the NVGs off and the false illusion of the black night and occasional red tracer round. With them on, it was just too much, giving me sensory overload.

'At some point in time during that run I collected a sense of overwhelming fate. It came down to training and doing what we were supposed to, and there was really no way to jink from everything being thrown at us. I just concentrated on the run and got into the "whatever happens, happens" mode.'

In 'Cutlass 44', Lt Cdrs Padilla and delaCruz were hastily preparing to release their ordnance. 'By the time we had started our attack run, there was only 15-20 seconds left before weapons release', explained Lt Cdr Padilla. 'I noticed AAA flashes in front of us and at "one o'clock" five seconds prior to me pickling the LGBs. I thought to myself that this was "G-time" (government time), and maintained delivery parameters. After delivery, I noticed that only one of our bombs had left the jet, so I did a post-release manoeuvre. I asked my RIO if the correct settings had been punched into the AWG-15, and he answered in the affirmative.

'After completing my post-release manoeuvre, I spotted AAA at "one o'clock", and very quickly assessed that it would not be a factor for our section. "Cutlass 43" then called out that they had seen more AAA from the airfield, as well as the launch of ballistic SAMs. I too had spotted the AAA, but not the SAMs. I then came back into the cockpit to check my flight parameters to ensure full support of the solitary LGB that we had dropped, and made appropriate adjustments and stayed on parameters for the next 17 seconds until the target was hit. "Good impact" was called, and "Cutlass 43" told us to flow onto a 190-degree heading.

'It was at this time that the complete gravity of the situation set in, as there was AAA around both aircraft from all directions. In fact there was

Both VF-14 and VF-41 flew CAP-only missions during the first 48 hours of OEF, and 'Fast Eagle 105' is seen here during one of those flights waiting its turn to tank from a 2nd Aerial Refueling Squadron/305th Air Mobility Wing KC-10A behind F/A-18Cs from VFA-15 and VFA-87. Lt Cdr David Lobdell led a CAP on 8 October;

'I was crewed up with Lt Skip Arny on the first night of the war, and we requested a CAP mission along the Afghan/Pakistan border due east of Gardez, as we figured that this would give us the best opportunity to claim a MiG-21 or Su-22, should one try to flee east. We made sure that our CAP area remained between ten and fifteen miles to the west of Pakistan so as to give us some intercept room should any jets decide to launch. Both F-14s in our section were configured exclusively in air-to-air mode, with two AIM-54Cs, two AIM-9Ls and a single AIM-7M. Although we performed a couple of positive ID runs on airliners transiting through the area, absolutely nothing launched from the various Afghan air bases. We had intel reports pre-war that indicated there were flyable aircraft in-country, but we soon realised that most of these jets had not flown in years. Nevertheless, CVW-8 and CVW-11 maintained a constant CAP in this area for the first few days of OEF' (*Cdr Brian Gawne*) enough light for us to plainly see "Cutlass 43" without the use of NVGs. Cdr Fecht called for a defensive manoeuvre against a SAM that was not seen by us until post-manoeuvre as "Cutlass 43" put out flares and acquired a streak of light drifting aft of their "five o'clock". At this time I engaged afterburner and accelerated to the south, continuously checking my belly and deploying countermeasures.'

The VF-14 crews had dropped three of their four LGBs on target.

CAVE BUSTING

As noted earlier in this chapter, VF-41's target on the opening night of the war was the entrance to a suspected al-Qaeda terrorist training camp in a mountain range southeast of Kandahar. A section of 'Black Aces" jets would be involved, with the lead machine crewed by squadron executive officer Cdr Pat Cleary and Lt Cdr Ed Meyle. The specialist GBU-24 Paveway III Penetrator LGB was chosen as the best weapon to ensure destruction of this challenging target, the 2000-lb bunker-buster boasting a hardened front casing that allowed the bomb to bore through five feet of concrete prior to detonating.

Just nine GBU-24s would be dropped by F-14s during OEF – four by VF-213, three by VF-14 and two by VF-41. The latter two units had used GBU-24s with limited success in Operation *Allied Force*, where the weapon's precise, and lengthy, flightpath, which ensured its steep, almost vertical, descent to the target, had proven difficult to achieve in hostile Balkan skies. With a conventional, more flexible, LGB such as the GBU-12, the RIO would typically lase the target for less than 30 seconds. However, in order to attain maximum penetration speed, the GBU-24 had to be released earlier and the target lased for 60 seconds.

The GBU-24 had a poor reputation within the Tomcat community, being dubbed 'pretty unreliable and a non-user-friendly weapon that doesn't have a high hit percentage' by VF-14 Operation *Allied Force* and OEF veteran Lt Cdr Van Kizer – he would get to drop a GBU-24 on a fuel/ammunition storage dump in Kabul on 17 October 2001. VF-41's Lt Cdr Scott Butler remembered that crews assigned GBU-24 missions had to spend 'hours weaponeering and target planning in order to ensure the accurate delivery of the bunker-buster. It's a labour-intensive weapon tailored exclusively for use against hardened targets, and fortunately for us, there weren't too many of those in Afghanistan'.

'Blacklion 111' (BuNo 161159) is marshalled towards one of CVN-70's waist catapults, the jet being armed with a single 2000-lb GBU-24A/B Paveway III LGB. Only a handful of these weapons were expended in OEF, VF-213 being the leading dropper with four. VF-41 made two GBU-24 attacks, with one being delivered by Lt Peter Gendreau and his RIO, Lt Cdr Scott Butler;

'We flew a daylight strike on a weapons storage facility on the outskirts of Kabul. Our target was a series of closely grouped bunkers in an area that had a high potential for collateral damage, and because of this, Lt Gendreau flew several runs at it just to make sure that we had our laser angled just right to achieve maximum weapon penetration. Our weapon definitely penetrated the bunker complex because we saw huge secondary explosions once it had detonated. That was the one drop that I did that made the nightly news back home' (*US Navy*)

VF-41 had its bunker-busting 'A team' leading the 8 October strike, with squadron CO Cdr Brian Gawne identifying Lt Cdr Ed Meyle as 'our GBU-24 expert'. Cdr Cleary described the mission to the Author;

'As the strike lead, I had to plan all the fuel for the jets involved, the tanker rendezvous points, the attack profiles for the target and the tactics we were to employ. Each of the VF-41 aircraft allocated to the mission was armed with just a single GBU-24 apiece, although the Tomcat was cleared to carry two. However, the pilot would have had to jettison one in order to get the aircraft down to landing weight should no bombs have been dropped during the course of the sortie. GBU-24s were simply too expensive to waste in this way.

'Relying exclusively on S-3 tanker support, we met a section of VS-31 jets that had launched ahead of us over Pakistan in order to top off our tanks, before pressing on into southern Afghanistan. With the target – a limestone cave dug into a mountain ravine – being some 40 miles to the southeast of Kandahar, we were out of SA-2 range.

'Unlike the SAM sites, which were defending key military bases in Kandahar, the terrorist camp was literally in the middle of nowhere. There were no lights to be seen anywhere on the ground, so we were dropping exclusively using the imagery generated by the LTS. When I looked out of the cockpit off NVGs, all around me was a sea of inky blackness. Although our GBU-24 guided well, we never saw it explode – this was the first bomb I had dropped in anger in 18 years of frontline flying. This was almost certainly because it had worked as advertised, penetrating deep into the side of the mountain before detonating.

'Having climbed up and away to the right in order to clear the target area to allow my wingman to make his attack run, I levelled off to see if anybody was shooting at us. Literally the whole mountainside was lit up with small-arms fire!

'During the return leg of the mission we again refuelled from two S-3s – this was the only organic strike flown by CVW-8 throughout OEF, with the USAF's sole input being its E-3 AWACS control.'

All three Tomcat units continued to strike fixed military targets over the next few days, as they worked through the CAOC-driven target sets supplied to them via the daily Air Tasking Order (ATO). Aside from bombing airfields, SAM sites, troop barracks and terrorist training camps, F-14 squadrons also escorted C-17s that flew humanitarian airdrop missions over Afghanistan from night one of OEF. Seven million Afghanis were 'at risk of loss of life as a result of the conditions inside Afghanistan' Gen Tommy Franks told the Senate Armed Services Committee in February 2002. The general also mentioned in his autobiography that he wanted the Afghan people to 'know that we are not attacking them, but that our war is with al-Qaeda and the Taleban'.

Relief drops were the best way to win 'hearts and minds' in Afghanistan, so humanitarian aid was despatched via C-17s flying marathon 6500-mile missions from Ramstein AFB, in Germany. Aerial refuelling en route, the Globemaster IIIs relied on F-14s to provide them with fighter protection while over enemy territory. Lt Cdr Will Pennington of VF-14 flew one of the first C-17 escort missions;

'The two C-17s that we were escorting were dropping leaflets and food over northern Afghanistan. For some reason the transports scheduled to deliver food to the locals the night before had had to turn back because their escorts had not showed up. This annoyed Gen Richard Myers, Chairman of the Joint Chiefs of Staff, and the Bush administration, which had publicly stated that aid was being dropped on a daily basis. Just minutes before we left the ready room to man our jets, we got a call from CAG, and my RIO went down to his office to talk with him. He was told that escorting C-17s was the most important thing that CVW-8 was going to do that day, and being a big deal, we weren't to screw it up!

'Having briefed as a division of four jets, we launched into the night, got our gas en route and then split up into two sections. We went one way in search of our C-17s and the other two F-14s went off somewhere else to find theirs. We rendezvoused with the transports south of the Afghan border and headed in-country. We maintained a figure-eight pattern above them so as to remain in position as they did their stuff at medium to low altitude at barely 220 knots – we trained to fly a similar profile when escorting CSAR helicopters. There was no threat as we escorted them in, and we watched the transports release their payloads through our FLIR, before shepherding them out of harm's way.

'In a moment of irony not lost on any of us, we then returned just a few minutes later to bomb a fixed target not 15 miles away from the C-17s' drop zone! It almost felt like we were baiting them to crush them. Of course, our respective payloads were meant for different "customers".'

TSTs AND FAC(A)s

Although both CVW-8 and CVW-11 hit pre-planned fixed targets for the first week of the war, the pursuance of TSTs such as al-Qaeda and Taleban leaders quickly assumed great importance. TST missions had initially been flown in Operation *Allied Force* against Serbian 'hide-and-seek' SAM launchers. In OEF, the targets were human, and they needed to be positively identified, tracked and then attacked typically in locations where collateral damage had to be kept to a minimum. The latter factor meant that F-14 units usually got the TST calls because the jet's LTS was far superior to the F/A-18's Lockheed Martin AAS-38B NITE Hawk pod when it came to breaking out targets in urban areas.

In the early stages of OEF, TSTs were often detected by CIA teams that had embedded themselves in Afghan cities soon after the 11 September attacks. Although needing to be hit as expeditiously as possible, TSTs often took hours to execute because of the multiple approval layers that the CAOC had to work through to authorise the delivery of an LGB, JDAM or Maverick missile from an aircraft, or a Hellfire missile from the newly-armed version of the MQ-1 Predator unmanned aerial vehicle (UAV). Tracking and assessment had to be done both by the CAOC at PSAB and by senior officers at CENTCOM HQ at MacDill AFB, in Tampa, Florida, via real time picture feeds from circling MQ-1s. The latter, based in Uzbekistan, were flown by both the USAF and the CIA, with the agency having operated UAVs over Afghanistan from the ex-Soviet Central Asian republic since mid-2000.

The tight rules of engagement stipulated by the Bush administration to prevent collateral damage often meant that TSTs had to be approved by President Bush or Secretary of Defense Rumsfeld, via CENTCOM commander Gen Franks. Such input from the top caused inevitable delays, and this in turn left naval aviators circling targets literally for hours on end as they waited for clearance to expend their ordnance.

Lt Marcus Lopez was one of eight naval aviators in VF-41 qualified to perform Forward Air Controller (Airborne) mission tasking in OEF. FAC(A) crews had to work out what were the bona fide targets by talking over the radio with CIA and SOF teams on the ground, liaising with airborne controllers and scouring the target area with their own systems. The Navy stipulates that only two-seat aircraft can perform the FAC(A) mission, and in OEF that meant the F-14 was the 'only game in town' when it came to flying this mission. Possessing the range, speed, targeting equipment, avionics and radios necessary to perform the demanding FAC(A) tasking, the Tomcat became the 'go to' platform for TST.

Lt Lopez described an early TST mission that he was involved in;

'My first FAC(A)-designated mission – although this ultimately evolved into a TST strike – was flown just three days after OEF started, when I got to work with one of the CIA FACs in-theatre. These guys weren't sufficiently trained to control TACAIR assets, and they were thin on the ground. Those in Afghanistan mostly operated around Kabul, seeking out TSTs. The CAOC specifically told CVW-8 that it wanted FAC(A) crews to go and work with the CIA "Spooks", as the latter lacked the experience necessary to provide jet crews with the kind of precise target coordinates required to attack key "pop up" targets in urban areas.

'This CIA-controlled TST operation in Kabul turned out to be one of my longest missions in OEF – I would subsequently discover that these sorties would typically last a hell of a long time. Things really dragged on as we waited for the CAOC and the FAC to give us the green light to drop our bombs. By the time my RIO and I landed back aboard the carrier, we had been airborne for almost nine hours.

'It turned out that the FAC had been waiting for key Taleban personnel to enter a tenement-style house that he was watching. He kept telling us to "wait a few more minutes", before having to go off-radio when people approached his position. He would then tell us where he was, and we could see him on the roofs of houses through the LTS as he moved from one location to another. We ended up having to tank twice while waiting for clearance to drop, until he was finally happy that all of the bad guys he was targeting were in the house for a meeting that he had received intel on. Only then were we passed target coordinates and cleared by him, and the CAOC via "Bossman", to drop a single GBU-12. The bomb went straight through the front door of the house.

'The FAC was very close to the target, his building being separated from it by a small park. Our bombing run had to be flown in such a way that we passed over this park and then aimed our LGB at the front of the house, so as to avoid inflicting collateral damage on nearby dwellings.

CTF-50's generic tanker force of S-3Bs supported TACAIR assets as best it could in OEF, as VS-29 (CVW-11) pilot Lt Mike Mrstik explained;

'The need for mission tankers required the launch of one S-3B for every two strike aircraft. Launching 15 minutes early, a section of Viking tankers would be joined later by a division of strike-fighters 100-150 nautical miles from the carrier. The six aircraft would then split into two divisions led by the S-3s, which would then proceed feet-dry over Pakistan en route to the USAF or RAF heavy tanker, or other assigned points. Each S-3 pumped 4000 lbs of fuel to each strike-fighter, before returning to the carrier. VS-29 aircraft routinely offloaded 90,000 lbs of fuel each day – an amount equal to the fuel carried by one-and-a-half KC-135s. The unit flew a total of 586 OEF missions' (*Lt Tony Toma*)

FAC(A)-qualified pilot Lt Marcus Lopez of VF-41 drew heavily on his Operation *Allied Force* experiences in OIF (*Lt Marcus Lopez*)

VF-41's 'Fast Eagle 103' (BuNo 158612) formates with a VF-14 jet during an OEF mission on 16 October 2001. This aircraft was the first production F-14 delivered to the Navy, being taken on strength on 12 May 1972. Based at Naval Air Test Center Patuxent River for many years, the fighter was passed on to Navy Reserve unit VF-201, at NAS Dallas, Texas, in the early 1990s. In 1997, it was one a handful of Reserve Tomcats returned to fleet use with VF-14 and VF-41, BuNo 158612 going on to see considerable action in Operation *Allied Force* in 1999 and in OSW and OEF in 2001. One of VF-41's six LTS jets on the latter cruise, it dropped 17 LGBs over Afghanistan. The aircraft was scrapped at NAS Oceana on 1 February 2002 as part of the Stricken Aircraft Reclamation and Disposal Program (SARDIP).

Note that the jet carries a name on its radome, its significance being explained by VF-41 CO, Cdr Brian Gawne. 'Some of our personnel wanted to paint nose art on our aircraft, but we didn't really have a suitable artist. In a bar in Palma, I found out our Maintenance Master Chief, AVCM Randy Bradley, had nicknamed the jets. He joked that he had 11 girlfriends, and had given each of the jets a girl's name. Once I heard this, I told AVCM Bradley to paint the names on the jets. Some crews were keen to have them named after their wives, but I asked them if they really wanted their buddies getting inside their wives, and they decided maybe that wasn't such a good idea!' (*Lt Cdr Van Kizer*)

'The LTS was critical in a mission such as this, as the Hornet's NITE Hawk pod was not powerful enough to break out urban targets with the required accuracy. The latter pod, from the height that we were operating at, would have been unable to distinguish one tenement house from another, let alone allow the pilot to count down the number of doors from the FAC's location to the target building, as we had to do.

'I had a wingman with me on this mission, and although he too worked up the target as we circled overhead Kabul, his primary role was to support us in any way he could. We always had a non-FAC(A) wingman for these sorties, and it was his job to watch over us should we have to descend below the 15,000-ft minimum altitude hard deck (introduced by CENTAF for OEF) in order to get our bombs, or someone else's, guided accurately to the target. Our wingman would remain above us in a position that allowed him to keep an eye on what was going on around us while we focused more closely on the target area.'

The increasing importance of FAC(A) crews signified a shift in the way the air war was now being prosecuted. VF-14 pilot Lt Mike Bradley chronicled this change as he saw it from a junior officer's perspective;

'The focus of the initial attacks was to ensure air superiority for all friendly forces, hence the targets we initially went after were air defence systems, strategic SAM sites, airfield complexes and aircraft. Kabul and Kandahar were common, popular targets. We also destroyed command and communication centres and terrorist training camps. Within days, however, we had expanded our scope to include emerging targets such as Taleban ground forces, tanks, vehicles and artillery, as well as TST.

'Most of my flights in OEF involved targeting tanks or armoured personnel carriers located in assigned "kill boxes" northwest of Kandahar. I also destroyed a SAM support truck and acquisition radar and a building complex being used for command/communication.

'From my perspective as a very junior officer, mission tasking was easy. Our flight schedule would be written per the ATO, with initial targets assigned. We would gather intel and imagery of our targets, along with that of many other possible flex targets, in CVIC. We would then brief, man up, launch and proceed in-country. After topping off on the tanker, we would check in with whoever happened to be the controlling agency that day (usually a USAF AWACS). They would then clear us to go after our assigned target, or give us a new one. We would then conduct our assignment, return to the tanker and either fly back to the ship or man a Defensive Counter Air CAP for a few hours, prior to heading home. A typical mission could last anywhere between 4.5 and 8.5 hours.'

With the emphasis shifting to mission flexibility to the extent where most TACAIR crews were now launching without knowing exactly what targets they were being sent against, those attributes that

made the F-14 the perfect FAC(A) platform also meant that the jet could perform the less specialised, but no less important, Strike Coordination and Reconnaissance (SCAR) role too. Indeed, FAC(A)-qualified RIO Lt John Kelly of VF-41 told the Author that he felt that most of the officially designated FAC(A) missions he flew were, in reality, SCAR sorties;

'The Navy has never been very good at handling the FAC(A) mission from an admin standpoint. No less than 95 percent of my ATO-fragged FAC(A) missions could have been labelled as SCAR, and the latter did not require a FAC(A)-qualified crew to perform them. When tasked with flying a FAC(A) mission, I would walk to the jet carrying a helmet bag filled with 15 to 20 target packs. We would have one or two targets pre-planned, and we knew that we would hit these early on in the sortie with the first strikers that checked in with us to service targets in our kill box. Such mission control saw us operating in the SCAR role, not as FAC(A)s.

'Typically, there were only four FAC(A) crews per unit in OEF, and we became so important that when we had to break off for fuel, the whole kill box would be declared shut by "Bossman" until we returned. Our wingman, who would remain on station, would not be allowed to handle incoming strikers because he and his RIO weren't FAC(A) qualified, yet most of the targets we were hitting were fixed in nature, and could have been lased by a competent crew with a serviceable LTS pod.

'Due to the emphasis placed on minimising collateral damage, an F-14 equipped with an LTS pod and a PTID was the "king" in OEF when it came to providing target identification. This sensor/display combination allowed us to pick out the target building that was the size of an outhouse, whereas our Hornet brethren could not repeat this performance without breaking the minimum altitude hard deck due to the poor resolution of their NITE Hawk pod. Providing visual and laser guidance to a Hornet pilot so that he could then hit a target with an LGB or LMAV (AGM-65E laser-guided Maverick missile) was effectively a SCAR mission.

'I can't blame the F/A-18C guys for being upset with me for lasing in their bombs, as I would have been upset too if I had been in their position. It simply boiled down to us having a better pod and associated displays when it came to satisfying the ROE for identifying targets in OEF.

'Technically, a mission should only be labelled FAC(A) when you are controlling air support for troops in contact, rather than hitting stationary targets with somebody else's ordnance. SCAR is more of a kill box mentality, where you are servicing fixed targets with assets that are cycled through under your control. Such missions are directed by AWACS controllers telling you which kill boxes to go and work in.

'When flying a SCAR mission – even though it might have been listed as a FAC(A) sortie – we would launch in a section along with a dedicated Prowler, and then pick up two or four strikers when we arrived in-country. We would drag them to the target area that we had been assigned either on the boat or by "Bossman". These strikers were usually other CVW-8 F-14s and F/A-18s, although they could just as easily have been jets from CVW-11 or USAF F-15Es or F-16s. We coordinated fuel for these assets once in-theatre, and then guided them to the target area.

'When the crews in this little strike package were all following the same game plan, and there were no conflicts within the jets as to who would hit what target and who was lasing ordnance for whom, things went well.'

Given the importance placed by the CAOC on FAC(A) crews, all three Tomcat units had to work hard to fulfil this requirement without having a detrimental effect on the flight schedule for non-qualified naval aviators. VF-14's official cruise report for OEF included the following entry, which explained how the unit dealt with the FAC(A) issue;

'The squadron creatively managed the daily combat flight schedule to increase the availability of critical FAC(A) qualified aircrews. Thoughtful scheduling enabled VF-14 to provide the maximum number of FAC(A)-qualified sections, and resulted in significantly enhanced effectiveness. In addition to aircrew management, aircraft were also configured to maximise lethality. Five aircraft were designated FAC(A) platforms and configured as "quadbombers". These jets provided a total of four LGBs to be delivered as "marks" by the FAC(A), and maximised the bringback capability. The remaining squadron aircraft were configured as "dual bombers". The combination of the FAC(A) with four GBU-12s and the escort with two GBU-16s resulted in unparalleled airborne flexibility.'

'DIAMONDBACKS" ENTER THE FRAY

The *Theodore Roosevelt* battle group arrived in the Northern Arabian Sea on 15 October, ostensibly to relieve the *Enterprise* battle group, which had had its deployment extended in the wake of the 11 September attacks. CVN-65 remained on station for a further week, ensuring a seamless turnover between CVW-8 and CVW-1. VF-41 sent two naval aviators to visit VF-102 as part of this turnover, and they explained what their unit had been doing in-country, as well as the administrative aspects associated with getting to and from Afghanistan. They showed aircrew the driveways that they had been using when heading through Pakistan, and briefed them on what tanker tracks were the most effective.

With this information to hand, VF-102's training officer set himself the task of single-handedly ensuring that no Tomcats from his unit flamed out during the ultra-long missions that the 'Diamondbacks' were about to fly. According to a junior officer in the squadron, 'his secret weapon was a kneeboard card that contained all the tanker frequencies given to him by CVW-8, the various tanker tracks and how much fuel it would take us to reach those tracks from known target areas in Afghanistan. The combination of the CVW-8 brief and the customised kneeboard cards meant that we were armed with some really sound information right from the start of our time in OEF'.

In the week prior to CVN-71 arriving off the coast of Pakistan, VF-102's training officer also met with his counterparts in the three Hornet units within CVW-1 (VMFA-251, VFA-82 and VFA-86) to discuss the future missions that they would be flying. He told the Author;

'We spoke about things like guiding LMAVs, which none of us had done before, the tactics and techniques we would employ when undertaking CAS in-theatre, and working with SOF teams – we had no idea where they would be, what kinds of radios they would be working with or the frequencies they would talking on. It was effectively trial by fire, and we just made it happen when we got into combat – we did not have a lot of guidance from on high in OEF. CAG placed few restraints on us when it came to getting the mission done. I have not experienced this level of freedom on subsequent war cruises.'

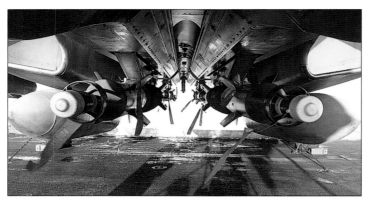

CVW-1 flew its first combat mission of OEF on the evening of 15 October when VF-102 was sent to attack a Taleban barracks complex north of Kandahar. Although both CVW-8 and CVW-11 had by now started to perform far fewer strikes on fixed, pre-briefed targets, the CAOC decided that CVW-1 needed to be introduced to OEF with a conventional pre-planned attack. Two F-14Bs from VF-102 led the first mission, with the RIO in the wingman's jet being the squadron's operations officer. He recalled that things did not go well on this strike right from the start;

'Our wing spoilers would not cycle in and out, but because it was so dark up on the flightdeck, both the final checkers on the catapult and I had failed to spot this. My pilot, who was also the squadron maintenance officer, immediately knew that they were inoperable, however, but he was determined not to miss this opening mission.

'Aside from no spoilers, when I checked my LTS pod after launching, I discovered that I was not getting any information from it in respect to weaponeering, including the provision of release times for our GBU-10s – I was getting a terrain picture, however. There were certain LTS functions that could only be tested once the jet was in the air, and it was then that I discovered the problem. I would have to manually calculate the weaponeering for our LGBs, taking into account our altitude and airspeed, so as to ensure that I released the bombs no earlier than X range and no later than Y range. These parameters would give the weapons the best chance of remaining in the laser energy "basket" all the way to the target.'

An LGB uses 'bang-bang' technology to hit its target, being guided through the acquisition of laser beam energy by its seeker head. The bomb travels up until it 'bangs' into the top edge of the beam rider and then the guidance vanes steer it back down until it strikes the bottom of the beam rider – this 'bang-bang' routine continues until the target is hit. Having corrected fully up or down, should the bomb then lose the beam because the designator has either been masked or the pod has gone out of range, it will follow the final input correction and miss the target by some considerable distance. An LGB is little more than a big glider, and it needs steering inputs to ensure that it hits the target.

'We had been tasked with attacking a previously bombed barracks just north of Kandahar airport, this target, I am certain, having been chosen for us by the CAOC in an effort to measure our combat capabilities', the operations officer continued. 'This first mission was in fact very similar to the whole Fallon training experience in work-ups, as I was given a target pack that provided me with photos and descriptions of the barracks.

'The lead jet in our section was flown by the skipper, with the CAG in the back seat. Although he ended up doing fine in subsequent missions, CAG was not quite up to the step tactically with the LTS at the beginning of OEF, and therefore failed to find the target on this first strike. We made four passes over it from the north to the south, during which time

All three Tomcat units involved in the opening phase of OEF adopted the four GBU-12 'quad bomber' loadout within days of the campaign commencing. 'Our teams could upload four GBU-12s in ten to fifteen minutes', recalled VF-213's 'gunner', CWO3 Michael Lavoie. 'Pre-war, I had planned on such a task taking 20-25 minutes to complete. Indeed, on previous cruises I had seen teams take 25 minutes to load a Phoenix, Sparrow and Sidewinder. During OEF, my guys were loading four bombs and chaff and flares in half the time!

'Our efforts were supported by other elements of the deck crew, and this meant that aircraft could be turned around in the shortest possible time. There were certain aspects of the rearming process that could be carried out while the aircraft was undergoing routine maintenance or being refuelled, for example. With forward-firing ordnance such as air-to-air missiles, you cannot touch it while the jet is being refuelled for fear that its electrical connection may short out and the round be fired off. This is not the case with bombs, however, which can be uploaded onto the racks by hand, as long as you are not fitting cartridge actuator devices or electrical connections. The F-14's belly-mounted ordnance pallets made rearming the jet more difficult than a Hornet, and the heat generated by the aircraft's engines during a six-hour flight proved hard to take. Things would get so hot back there that a four- to six-man team working in close proximity with one another would be showering in each other's sweat!' (US Navy)

I tried my best to get his eyes onto the target with my degraded FLIR, but to no avail. CAG and the CO ended up having to jettison a bomb on their way back to the ship and landing with the other one still under the jet.

'As we ran in on our fourth, and last, pass, I was working hard trying to get CAG locked onto the target and our bombs off too, as by now we were running critically low on fuel. I said to my pilot, who had flown Intruders in *Desert Storm*, to standby to "pickle", and he questioned whether we had the barracks targeted correctly. This split-second delay in him hitting the release button meant that the bombs left the jet a tenth-of-a-mile too late. Lacking any laser energy to ensure accurate guidance, the GBU-10s missed the target by about a mile according to the Bomb Hit Assessment (BHA) tapes we viewed back on the ship.

'Undoubtedly my luckiest moment in OEF came when these LGBs exploded in open ground, rather than amongst houses. These were the only bombs of the 44 I dropped in OEF that failed to hit the target.

'The second section of jets that launched shortly after us enjoyed no more success than we had done, being let down by a tanker no-show and having to divert to the air base at Jacobabad, in Pakistan – there were really only enough big wing tankers in-theatre for two air wings at that time. Both Tomcats had just 4000 lbs of gas apiece left in their tanks when they landed. We were all "shining our asses" as a squadron during the first couple of nights in OEF.'

After this shaky start, VF-102 soon dialled itself into the mission. Indeed, by the time CVN-71 out-chopped from OEF in early March 2002, the 'Diamondbacks' had delivered more ordnance – 420,000 lbs, plus 50,000 lbs buddy-lased for other platforms – and flown more combat hours (5000+) than any other Tomcat unit in the campaign.

Four days after VF-102's combat debut, the first SOF teams were inserted into Afghanistan. The ground war was about to begin in earnest.

VF-102's colour jet (BuNo 163225) cruises over typically inhospitable terrain as it heads north towards Afghanistan soon after the unit had arrived in the Northern Arabian Sea. Built by Grumman in early 1989, this aircraft was issued to VF-24 in May of that year. Later serving with VF-101 and VF-103, the jet was assigned to VF-102 in 1998. It remained with the unit until transferred to VF-101 when the 'Diamondbacks' received F/A-18Fs in May 2002. BuNo 163225 was claimed by SARDIP in August 2004.

Like all of VF-102's ten-strong fleet of F-14Bs, this aircraft was worked hard during the unit's 159-day stretch on the line. 'Our jets stood up to the rigours of the cruise pretty well, and we usually had six F-14s up on the roof at the start of the day's flying programme', recalled one of the unit's pilots. 'We also went the extra mile and spared every launch cycle that we had jets committed to. This meant that we always had three crews dialled into the mission so that there was a spare available should a primary jet go down mechanically. Although this placed a great strain on our maintenance folks, VF-102 still finished third in CVW-1 for jet availability on cruise, beaten only by VMFA-251 and VFA-82' (*VF-102*)

GROUND WAR

The early stages of OEF had progressed well, with TACAIR assets from carriers in the Northern Arabian Sea, supported by USAF heavy bombers, having hit hundreds of targets all over Afghanistan. The country's rudimentary air defence system had been attrited, with all major airfields rendered inoperable and all known SAM sites knocked out. AAA and MANPADS still posed a threat, but only if strike aircraft dropped below the theatre-wide 15,000-ft hard deck limit. Tanker and AWACS issues had also been worked out, thus allowing jets from three carriers to conduct round-the-clock missions in-country.

Yet despite achieving total air superiority and dropping tens of thousands of tons of bombs, seemingly little progress had been made on the ground. Northern Alliance leaders were keen to take the fight to the Taleban, but they felt that the air campaign was stuck on hitting fixed targets. VF-41's Lt Cdr David Lobdell shared these frustrations, as his unit seemed to be bombing the same targets over and over again;

'We attacked the key Afghan airfields several times over in the early stages of OEF, for example. Indeed, it seemed like every third night I was bombing targets at the air base on the outskirts of Kabul. The CAOC clearly wanted every last aircraft at these sites destroyed, despite our video BHA indicating that the Afghan air force had not flown these machines in a number of years. This was frustrating for us, as we could only hit those targets that appeared on the approved list issued to us by the CAOC. It was not a "free-for-all go out and hit what you want" situation in OEF. We knew that the Northern Alliance was anxious that we bomb other targets aside from air bases and SAM sites, but the ground communications in-theatre at the time were not robust enough for us to safely give them the close air support that they were so desperately requesting. This came later once the SOF teams were inserted.'

By mid-October the Bush administration was having to field criticism of the way OEF was progressing, prompting Donald Rumsfeld to tell the press 'we're making some progress in our efforts to create the conditions for sustained anti-terrorist operations inside Afghanistan'. To that end, the first attacks against frontline Taleban troops defending cities such as Kabul and Mazar-e-Sharif had been conducted on 16 October.

Ultimately, however, OEF had been underway almost a month before the Northern Alliance started to seize the initiative on the ground. It had taken a while for the carrier air wings to adjust to this new style of persistent air power, whereby they had to perform 24-hour operations. Each air wing would be responsible for manning a 12-hour shift, and in that time they could expect to tally 70 to 80 launches.

But air power alone would not win OEF. Gen Tommy Franks knew full well that he needed 'American boots on the ground. The sooner we had the SOF teams' combat air controllers designating Taleban and al-Qaeda targets for bombers, the quicker Northern Alliance troops could climb out of their World War 1-style trenches and advance on the enemy'. CENTCOM's plan called for 200 SOF personnel to help the Northern Alliance initiate combat operations in the early days of OEF.

Getting opposition forces to this point took time, however, as they were far from ready to take advantage of coordinated air strikes when OEF commenced. SOF teams had to create a working relationship with individual opposition leaders, and vast sums of money changed hands in an effort to expedite this process. Secretary of State Colin Powell summed the situation up perfectly in an interview with *The Washington Post* on 25 November 2001 when he stated 'You had a First World air force and a Fourth World army, and it took a while to connect the two'.

Admittedly, the CIA had been working in the field with various Northern Alliance leaders for months by the time OEF started, but it would take SOF teams on the ground to direct military operations in-theatre. Getting these teams into Afghanistan immediately after 7 October turned into a logistical nightmare for CENTCOM, which Gen Franks subsequently described as 'ten days of hell' in his autobiography.

Poor weather initially blighted attempts to insert SOF teams, with dust storms and snow obliterating landing sites for several days running. The State Department was also experiencing difficulties in getting Uzbek government approval for the use of several key bases as staging posts for SOF insertion. Finally, the CIA had told CENTCOM that the Northern Alliance could not guarantee the safety of any SOF personnel that did link up with them should operations against the Taleban not go according to plan. Such remarks only served to confirm the Pentagon's view that the Northern Alliance was little more than a mercenary organisation that would fight the war when it chose to do so, and not under US command.

On 15 October President Bush pressed Gen Franks for an update on CENTCOM's efforts to get SOF teams in-theatre, as he had promised would be done expeditiously once OEF started. At that time, not a single team had made it into Afghanistan, and the commander-in-chief was not at all pleased to hear this. Within four days of the president indicating to Gen Franks that he needed to get US troops in-country as soon as possible, two USAF Special Operations Command (USSOCOM) MH-53Js flew Army Special Forces A-Team 555 from Jacobabad, in Pakistan, to a landing zone in the Shamali plains, just north of Kabul.

Part of Task Force (TF) Sword, A-Team 555, and their attached USAF combat controllers, would provide the 'eyes on target' for the SOF-centric phase of OEF that would ultimately lead to the ousting of the Taleban from power. By the end of October, four teams (some from TF Dagger, established at Karshi-Kanabad air base, in Uzbekistan) had been inserted, as well as two battalion-level units. Their composition numbered just 78 personnel, and they were supported by CIA teams Alpha, Echo and Jawbreaker. There were also British and Australian SAS/SBS personnel in-country too, controlled by TF Sword/Dagger.

Shortly after the SOF teams arrived, the CAOC divided Afghanistan up into 30 engagement zones (or kill boxes) so as to facilitate the quick vectoring of TACAIR assets against emerging TSTs. This was a critical development now that there were friendlies on the ground, as the CAOC had no experience of dealing with SOF/CIA controllers in combat.

Having been dropped off just inside the Afghan border by the USSOCOM MH-53Js, SOF teams were then shuttled all over the country in Mil-8/17 'Hip' helicopters similar to the type that had been used by the CIA from September. The secrecy surrounding the SOF teams' movements meant that none of the air wings were aware that these ex-Russian helicopters were being flown in-country by friendly forces. The Taleban had a large fleet of Mil helicopters that had previously been flown by the Afghan air force following the Soviet withdrawal in 1989, and naval aviators had been specifically told that they were forbidden from engaging any helicopter without CAOC approval. However, it seems that only good fortune prevented the SOF/CIA transports from being misidentified as hostile and downed by prowling jets in OEF.

VF-41 pilot Lt(jg) Shawn Price was just one of a number of naval aviators to have a close encounter with an unidentified Mil-8/17;

'While flying one of CVW-8's final OEF missions, Lt(jg) Steve Winfield and I were on station during a rare daylight sortie when we were given some real-time tasking to go and find a helicopter spotted near Jalalabad. "Bossman" had contacted us while we were tanking, and I had turned my primary radio down so that I could focus on staying in the KC-135's basket – not an easy thing to do in a heavy F-14A at high altitude. When I left the tanker and headed towards our previously assigned target area, my RIO told me that we had been given another target to hit. This came as a total surprise to me, as I had heard none of his conversation with "Bossman" because I had had my radio turned down!

'My RIO quickly filled me in on the target details, explaining how "Bossman" had told him that CENTCOM had been chasing this particular helicopter for almost three weeks! Once in the target area, my section lead and I made a solitary "fishing" run with our LTS, and my RIO eventually spotted the Mil-8 on the ground. Unfortunately, my LTS display screen in the front cockpit had failed soon after we left the tanker, so Lt(jg) Winfield had to talk my eyes onto the target. Although I failed to physically spot it – and neither did my Tomcat section lead – my RIO had the helicopter locked up with the LTS and destroyed it with an LGB.

'Just seconds before the bomb hit the helicopter, our section lead shouted over the radio "DON'T DROP, DON'T DROP". By then there was nothing we could do to change the direction of the weapon. Having not been able to actually see the target that we were bombing through the LTS, and without a back-up identification from my flight lead, I had asked my RIO several times prior to pickling the GBU-12 whether it was indeed the helicopter that "Bossman" had cleared us to attack. He confirmed this every time. We had captured good BHA footage to support our attack, and we were anxious to clear this matter up as soon as we got back to the ship.

'Worried sick that we had just bombed some of our own troops, there was little conversation in the jet as we headed south towards the carrier. Having trapped back

'Fast Eagle 104' (BuNo 158630) heads north on one of the unit's last OEF missions. From this angle, its 'quad bomber' configuration can be clearly seen. F-14 crews from CVW-8 usually expected to drop all their bombs, as VF-41 RIO Lt John Kelly explained to the Author;

'My abiding memory of OEF was the sheer amount of ordnance that we got through in just a matter of days. On one particular night mission, Lt Marcus Lopez and I lased so many LMAVs and GBU-12s that we forgot that we still had an LGB on our jet! As usual, I was reviewing the mission tape for BHA during our three-hour transit back to the ship when I told him that I could only find film for three of our four bombs. He was as surprised as I was!

'I selected the bomb release switch in the rear cockpit so as to double check that we did indeed still have a GBU-12 on the jet, and Lt Lopez got a hot trigger switch to confirm that there was an LGB on one of the rails. We immediately told the CO when we got back, and made sure that the armourers knew that there was nothing wrong with the bomb. He asked us why we hadn't dropped it, and I replied that we had lased so many damned Mavericks and other peoples' LGBs that we had forgotten we had one of our own left – we preferred to keep hold of our bombs for as long as possible just in case we had to quickly hit a target. Cdr Gawne asked me how many we had lased in, and a check of my mission card revealed 16 LMAVs and some GBU-12s' (*Cdr Brian Gawne*)

The crew of 'Blacklion 103' (BuNo 163899) fly a flag sent to them by officers serving in the New York City Police Department. Photographed in late October 2001, the aircraft already boasts a lengthy bomb tally beneath its cockpit. This aircraft would duly see more action with VF-213 in OIF (*Lt Tony Toma*)

The AGM-65E Laser Maverick missile proved hugely popular in OEF, as Lt Marcus Lopez of VF-41 recalled. 'As a FAC(A), I preferred to work with the LMAV, as it was more accurate than an LGB. It truly was a "shoot and scoot" weapon for the F/A-18 when terminally guided by an F-14, as the pilot simply fired the missile and left – we did all the targeting for the LMAV with our LTS. The smoke plume from its rocket motor made the missile clearly visible to the F-14 crew. You could also move the LTS spot from target to target with ease even with the weapon in flight, as the LMAV always followed the laser energy. You didn't have such flexibility with an LGB, although the GBU-12 was quite manoeuvrable' (*US Navy*)

aboard, we had barely climbed out of the jet when CAG Ops officer Lt Cdr Bill Lind congratulated us on destroying the helicopter that CVW-8 had been chasing since the start of OEF! Words cannot adequately describe how relieved we were to hear that. The validity of the target had been confirmed by our BHA film of the Mil-8 being struck by our LGB.'

FIRST SOF OP

The air wings felt the effect of having SOF teams in-country almost immediately, as emerging targets in special zones and engagement areas could be quickly identified by them. The very first SOF target to be hit was the compound of Taleban leader Mullah Omar, which was attacked on the night of 19 October 2001 – just hours after the first A-Team 555 had been inserted. VF-213 RIO Lt Cdr Michael Peterson and his pilot, Lt John Saccomando, played a key role in this operation.

'We were part of a mixed section of one F-14D FAC(A) and an escort F/A-18C, piloted by Lt Cdr Rey Molina, that was tasked with controlling air wing CAS assets in support of a SOF raid on the home of Mullah Omar on the outskirts of Kandahar', explained Lt Peterson.

'Mullah Omar lived in a highly-guarded compound shaped like a diamond and protected by high walls. The SOF package consisted of several helicopters, including ground force transports and gunships, two AC-130 Spectre gunships in an orbit directly over the objective and a "CAS stack" of strike fighters offset to the side of the compound. The concept was to cover the insertion, operation and extraction of the SOF units with fire support from helicopter gunships and the AC-130s inside the compound, with the additional firepower of the air wing assets to address threats outside the compound. There were several Joint Tactical Air Controllers (JTACs) and SOF FACs with the ground element, an overall airborne controller and our mixed F-14 and F/A-18 section all operating together, so radio discipline was essential.

'Our launch, initial tanking and flight en route to the rendezvous point was uneventful. We were carrying two CBU-99 Rockeye cluster

bomb units, and intended to buddy-lase for Hornets from our air wing, these aircraft being armed with LGBs and LMAVs. As a FAC(A) crew, we were allowed to share control of the airspace over the target area with the other JTACs due to our supposed higher levels of situational awareness and comms with all the "players" involved. We wanted to use stand-off weapons from the CAS stack as much as possible so as to deconflict air wing jets from the fires of the AC-130s directly overhead the compound.

'At first things were pretty calm, as the various packages checked in on station and we waited for the helicopter assault force to arrive. During this lull in the action we left the primary SOF FAC on scene to cover the initial force insertion while we headed to the tanker to top off our fuel. We wanted to be able to stay on station if needed during the actual insertion period, so we planned on tanking up front in the operation.

'As we headed to the KC-135, we monitored the primary controlling frequency so that we could keep a check on the progress of the operation. We could hear the initial kick off and arrival of the SOF troops as we refuelled. By the time we had topped off and got back on station to join the fight, all hell had broken loose inside the compound. The helicopters had dropped off the SOF elements that were now entering the compound and engaging in several firefights with the guards. Tracers and gunfire were visible on NVGs both inside and outside the compound and into the surrounding hills. You could hear the automatic weapons fire in the background as controllers made frantic requests for, and directed, fires.

'A ZSU-23-4 armoured, mobile AAA piece was then spotted heading down from the hills north of the compound, firing at the helicopters orbiting near it. The firehose of tracers was clearly visible on our NVGs, and Lt Saccomando quickly set up to put the target in the centre of our HUD so as to acquire it with the LTS and direct an attack against it.

'However, before we got the chance to set up an attack, one of the AC-130 gunships opened up on the AAA piece with its 40 mm cannon and completely destroyed the gun – a good secondary explosion was also seen emanating from the target. Viewing this attack through the NVGs was one of the most impressive examples of destructive firepower I have ever witnessed. The crew manning the AAA piece had probably only got off three bursts of fire in total prior to being taken out by the AC-130.

'We heard several controllers calling for CAS inside the compound, and it was hard to get a word in on the radio. They were, understandably, very excited, but the FAC(A)s on station had to make sure that we got an accurate description of the target, and that friendly forces would not be caught up in the effects, before directing fires in close proximity to them. Knee-jerk responses to requests could have easily resulted in fratricide.

'We eventually received a call to take out a guard tower on the compound wall that was delivering fire into the compound itself. Setting up for an attack, we confirmed with the SOF controller on the ground which tower it was he wanted destroyed, then instructed our Hornet wingman to turn in toward the compound while we dialled the laser code for his weapons into our LTS. We located the guard tower, designated it with laser energy and told Lt Cdr Molina to call "good spot" when his LMAV had acquired the target. The LMAV was the perfect weapon to take out the guard tower, for not only did it contain a 300-lb shaped-charge warhead, but it would safe up, climb and dud well down range if it lost laser energy during the time of flight. This feature was incredibly valuable when it came to protecting friendly forces.

'Lt Cdr Molina called "good spot" and we cleared him "hot" on the tower as we arced across the target, lasing out the right side of our aircraft where the LTS pod was located. A moment later, the cockpit filled with light. All the aircraft involved in this operation were flying around with their lights off, and we were using altitude deconfliction to avoid a collision. Our wingman was passing right above us as we cleared him "hot", and the LMAV's rocket motor lit up our entire cockpit as it headed downrange towards the target. We continued to lase the guard tower until the LMAV scored a direct hit, to the cheers of the SOF forces on the radio. They then directed us to take out the remaining guard tower on the opposite side of the compound, which we destroyed using the same tactics.

'While this was going on, there were skirmishes occurring inside the compound and in the high terrain that surrounded the target area to the north. Helicopter gunships were also trying to suppress a large amount of fire being delivered into the compound from heavy-calibre weapons sited on the ridgeline to the north, but they were also vulnerable to these guns too, so we were directed to drop a string of Rockeye on the ridgeline.

'We avoided the AC-130 line-of-fire and descended to set up our Rockeye run. As Lt Saccomando pressed in toward the ridgeline for a level lay down delivery, I cued the LTS out in front of us to capture the effects of the combined 494 Mk 118 bomblets contained in our CBU-99s.

'Each of the units was fitted with a FMU-140 DPF (dispenser proximity fuse), which could be set with an arming time and a height-of-function (HOF) trigger that would detect the CBU-99's height above the target and then open the dispenser to produce an optimum cluster weapon footprint on the ground. F-14A/Bs did not generate sufficient ballistic information via their elderly weapons computers to effectively employ the FMU-140 DPF fitted to the CBU-99. The F-14D, however, had a more modern stores management system that collated accurate ballistics and allowed the aircrew to enter the HOF for the FMU-140.

'The CBU-99 was a deadly weapon against tanks and APCs, and was equally as effective against troops if they were travelling in a soft-skinned vehicle such as a truck or SUV. Very few Rockeyes were dropped in OEF, however, as the unfortunate side effect of this weapon is that unexploded cluster munitions are left behind due to the high dud rate suffered by the bomblets when dropped on soft soil. This became a real problem if friendly troops planned to occupy the area at any point following CBU use, as they could later set off the bomblets if disturbed.

'Seconds before we reached the release point, while scanning the target area through our LTS, we saw a helicopter strafing the same ridgeline. We immediately aborted our attack and pulled away. In all the confusion on the radio, the crew of the helicopter had missed the fact that they had a Tomcat bearing down on the ridgeline, and had failed to leave the area.

'The rest of the operation seemed to go smoothly after this, with SOF forces eliminating any remaining resistance and then re-boarding the transport helicopters in preparation for their exfiltration from the area. There were still targets external to the compound when we handed over to the next wave of controlling F-14 FAC(A)s from CVW-8, and they cleaned them up and then covered the SOF helicopter egress.

'Before Lt Saccomando and I flew back to the carrier, we were able to head to a nearby predetermined alternate target area – a vehicle staging depot east of Kandahar – and expend our Rockeyes on military trucks and APCs that were parked in close formation. The CBU-99s produced a spectacular pattern on the ground, as well as several secondary explosions. These were the only cluster-bomb units dropped by VF-213 in OEF.'

Attacks such as this one convinced Northern Alliance leaders that air strikes could indeed influence the situation on the ground in their favour, as air power started to shift its emphasis from fixed targets to emerging frontline ones. SOF teams kept TACAIR assets busy as they rooted out Taleban armour and troop concentrations defending Afghan cities.

'BIG E' HEADS HOME

On 23 October 2001, just as the focus of the air war shifted, CVN-65 and CVW-8 chopped out of the Northern Arabian Sea and headed home. The vessel had been on deployment since 25 April, and having been extended for a month, the ship's company, as well as the personnel of CVW-8, were relieved to be Virginia-bound. Both F-14 units had been given a brief glimpse of the direction in which the air war was now heading, and they were not impressed, as Lt Marcus Lopez recalled;

'Two days before we left OEF, I returned to the boat without having dropped my bombs for the first time in the conflict. It was at that point I knew it was time to go home. By then, crews were no longer regularly bombing targets on every mission. The air war had changed from fixed target strikes to battlefield support, as the ground war began to ramp up. Now, it was a case of if you were needed you would be called by "Bossman" to check in with a JTAC (Joint Terminal Attack Controller) and expend your ordnance on his say so.

'Things had progressively got more structured as the war had gone on, and with more friendly troops now on the ground, there was no flexibility being given to TACAIR crews when it came to looking for targets to bomb. When I was flying those early missions as a FAC(A), I could pick my own targets, work out how best to attack them and then get other jets in to drop ordnance. This had all changed by the time we left.'

Although only committed to OEF for the first 16 days of the campaign, VF-41 had dropped a staggering 200,000 lbs of precision-

The officer cadre of VF-41 pose for their end of cruise photograph during CVN-65's brief three-day port call to Souda Bay, in Crete, in late October 2001. Following the 'Black Aces'' history-making Operation *Allied Force*/OSW cruise in 1999, when the unit dropped more than 200,000 lbs of ordnance, the 2001 deployment could have been something of an anti-climax for the crews involved. However, brief action in OSW and 16 breathless days of combat in OEF ensured that VF-41 once again led the way as the squadron became embroiled in the Global War on Terror. Despite the unit being equipped with aircraft that were, in the main, destined to be scrapped once the cruise was over, the pilots and NFOs seen here again dropped more than 200,000 lbs of ordnance (all LGBs), with most of this being expended between 8 and 23 October.

'VF-41 achieved an 82 per cent PGM hit rate, which was a level of accuracy that had never previously been achieved by the US Navy', unit CO Cdr Brian Gawne told the Author. 'My operations officer calculated that our pilots and RIOs would have flown 60+ hours in a single month had we been kept on station beyond the 16 days CVW-8 was committed to OEF. We would have required a waiver to keep this sortie rate up, as the Navy states that 50 hours is the most you can fly in a month without official approval. We ended up with an average of 116 traps per pilot by the end of the cruise' (*Cdr Brian Gawne*)

guided munitions (202 LGBs) in that time. Sister-squadron VF-14 achieved equally impressive statistics during this period, expending 174 LGBs totalling 179,324 lbs. Its crews also buddy-lased 28 LMAVs and 23 LGBs for other TACAIR assets. These numbers had been achieved flying 22 of the oldest F-14As in service. Yet despite the age of their jets, neither unit had diverted a Tomcat ashore.

CVN-71/CVW-1 would replace CVN-65/CVW-8 on the night page, having been conducting missions since 15 October.

By month-end, following a fortnight of battlefield preparation by TACAIR assets, Northern Alliance military leader Mohammed Fahim Khan informed Gen Franks that his forces were ready to advance on the key northern towns of Taloqan, Kunduz and Mazar-e-Sharif. He told the CENTCOM boss 'your air forces should concentrate its bombing to allow our forces to take these cities. Then I will move south to Bagram'(the ex-Soviet air base in Kabul).

Like sister-squadron VF-41, VF-14 also matched its 1999 exploits during the unit's final Tomcat cruise in 2001. Indeed, according to the unit's official cruise report, 'Under the leadership of five designated Strike Leads, VF-14 led more strikes than any other squadron in CVW-8 during two theatres of operation'. The 'Tophatters' dropped 174 LGBs, totalling 179,324 lbs, and buddy-lased 28 LMAVs and 23 LGBs during OEF. And like VF-41, it did this flying the oldest F-14s in the fleet (_VF-14_)

The colour jets from VF-41 and VF-14 lead the 22-aircraft formation fly-in to NAS Oceana at the end of the squadrons' final cruise with the Tomcat on 9 November 2001 (_Lt Cdr Van Kizer_)

The destruction of emerging targets during XCAS (the CAOC's moniker for immediate close air support missions) became increasingly important as the Northern Alliance girded itself for action. In order to perform these missions, the ATOs emanating from PSAB assigned F-14s and F/A-18s from CVW-1 and CVW-11 with specific vulnerability times that tied in with the operational schedules of their carriers. During these 'vul times', jets had to be available in-theatre, with an appropriate mix of ordnance, ready to undertake mission tasking given to them by the CAOC (via AWACS controllers) or from ground controllers.

Typically, requests for air strikes came from SOF team controllers via their Air Control Elements (ACE) attached directly to SOF Task Forces working from locations in Afghanistan. The ACE would contact the

Special Operations Liaison Element (SOLE) at the CAOC, who would in turn talk with co-located CENTAF operations directors. Finally, the latter would radio the on-station AWACS, and its crew of combat controllers would vector jets to the target. Occasionally, 'Bossman' controllers would have the SOF FACs talk directly with the strikers, although their interface with TACAIR assets did not always work.

VF-102 conducted more XCAS and FAC-assisted strikes than any other F-14 unit in OEF, with many of its crews flying 60+ missions during CVN-71's run of 159 days on the line in combat. Therefore, naval aviators such as the unit's training officer were well qualified to pass judgment on the abilities of the ground controllers in-theatre;

'The SOF guy running most of the ground controlling around Kandahar was good, but his counterparts in Bagram and Mazar-e-Sharif sucked. In the main, they were young enlisted guys who had received only cursory ground FAC training as part of their overall SOF syllabus, the latter seemingly leaving them as jack-of-all-trades and master of none. We wasted too much time on the radio trying to find the target that the FAC wanted hit, as he would be describing it to us as he saw it from the ground, rather than trying to view it from our elevated perspective.

'As a perfect example of what we had to deal with, during the fight to take Mazar-e-Sharif, my RIO and I were trying to work through a target talk-on being given to us by a FAC just south of the city. After 30 minutes of this, we confirmed with him that we could see the road in the valley that we thought he was describing. Believing we had it suitcased, my RIO asked the FAC if he could see the target from his position? The FAC replied, "No. I'm looking at my evasion chart"! We thought that he had had his eyes on the damn target all this time. Luckily this was not a TST, and from that day onward the first thing I asked the FAC when I checked in with him was "are you looking at the target?" If he replied in the negative, and stated he was studying his TPC (Tactical Pilotage Chart), we would endeavour to pull out the same chart and look over it too. We always carried a number of these charts for southern and eastern areas of the country, but we had little TPC coverage for the north or west.

'Such unprofessional talk-ons affected the Hornet pilots far more than us Tomcat crews, as factors such as the jet's short range, its poor targeting pod and only one set of eyes in the cockpit meant that they would run out of fuel long before they had located the target being described to them by the FAC. This was the primary reason why VF-102 tried to take control of the airspace overhead the target area whenever possible, and then work through the pain of the target talk-on with the FAC. Once we had the target suitcased, only then would we call the Hornets in from the tanker to deliver their ordnance. Experienced Hornet guys would, of course, prefer to find the target themselves, and we were happy for them to do so.

'I regularly buddy-lased for the Hornet units in CVW-1, and in my experience the Marines of VMFA-251 were the best to work with. They simply wanted to get their ordnance on target as expeditiously as possible. The Marine pilots would check in and ask us if we could see the target. If we replied in the affirmative, they would say "go ahead and lase it for me" without any further questions asked. There was no issue about lasing their own weapon, as they were happy to put their LGB or LMAV in the laser basket as directed by us, and then let us terminally guide it home.

'The opposite was true for a few of the Navy light strike pilots in our air wing, who always wanted to lase their own targets. I would tell them in pre-mission briefs, "If you are 100 percent sure that you have the right target locked up with your NITE Hawk pod, then go ahead and hit it. If you have just one percent doubt whether you are locked onto the right target or not, or you cannot capture it with your laser, then just give it to us, because if you do drop your weapon and it misses, then I am going to give you a hard time in the debrief!"

'There were a couple of Hornet guys who felt that it was unacceptable that their weapons would be guided onto targets by someone in another aircraft. I remember watching these individuals miss a few aim points during OEF. These were usually "old school" Hornet pilots who would assure me on their run in to the target that they had it locked up with their pod, so they didn't need our help. Clearly they did, as their bombs would sometimes miss by up to 1000 ft.'

Despite these problems, VF-102 offered the Northern Alliance critical air support as it closed on Mazar-e-Sharif. The fighting surrounding this northern city was some of the fiercest of OEF, as the Taleban were fully aware of Mazar-e-Sharif's strategic significance. Land routes from Uzbekistan into northern Afghanistan all passed through the city, and the Coalition needed to secure these roads in order to allow military and humanitarian bulk loads to flow into the country via truck convoys. Targets selected by ground controllers and serviced via XCAS had really become the order of the day by early November.

'KNIFE 03' DOWN

During the pre-dawn hours of 3 November, a USAF Task Force Dagger MH-53J, call-sign 'Knife 03', crashed in mountainous terrain near Nawoor, south of Kabul. The helicopter was one of a pair that had been despatched from Jacobabad air base on a medevac mission to extract a gravely ill soldier from SOF A-Team 555. The helicopters encountered high winds and dust en route, and the lead MH-53 bounced off an unseen 10,000-ft peak and crashed in the snow. All 11 crewmen survived, although some were injured, and the second helicopter quickly rescued them. The damaged MH-53 could not be flown out, so it was decided to destroy it in situ with an LGB. That job was given to VF-102, and the Author interviewed the pilot who undertook the mission;

'I just happened to be manning the Rescue Mission Command alert duty that morning, and we launched into the night sky and raced to the area where the MH-53 had come down. There were already two Hornets on station that had been diverted from a patrol, and we arrived just as the second helicopter was picking up the survivors and preparing to depart the scene of the crash.

'We initially had a hard time finding the downed MH-53 because no one seemed to have definitive coordinates that they could give us. Once we had located the helicopter, it then took a long time for us to be granted approval to destroy it. We initially escorted the remaining helicopter out of Afghanistan, before returning to the crashed MH-53 and hitting it with a single LGB. With the helicopter still being full of fuel when it crashed, the GBU-12 started a ferocious fire, which totally consumed the MH-53.

'Upon returning to the ship, we watched a CNN report that showed local villagers jumping up and down on the charred wreckage of the helicopter – that was a surreal moment!'

GO FOR YOUR GUN

On 5 November the Northern Alliance at last began to take ground from Taleban and al-Qaeda forces to the south of Mazar-e-Sharif. As expected, enemy forces proved difficult to shift from their well-prepared defensive positions, and Hornets and Tomcats from CVW-11 were soon called in by SOF controllers to winkle them out. Amongst the jets on station performing XCAS was 'Blacklion 101', crewed by squadron CO Cdr Chip King and Lt Cdr Michael Peterson. VF-213's boss recalled;

'We were the last section on station, and had already dropped all of our ordnance and exited the target area. We continued to monitor the frequency as we made our way to the tanker. We heard a frantic call for more ordnance from "Tiger", who we had just worked with. We quickly headed back to his location, informing him that all we had remaining was 600 rounds of 20 mm SAFHEI (semi-armour piercing high explosive incendiary ammunition), and given the current Special Instructions for OEF, we were unable to descend to an altitude that would allow our strafing attacks to be effective. The urgency in his voice was obvious, and the AWACS responded for us to standby as Lt Cdr Peterson made several attempts to get clearance for us to get below the hard deck.

'We located the closest Northern Alliance position with our FLIR and set ourselves up for an immediate attack if cleared. You could see that the friendlies were being overrun by enemy troops mostly on horseback and in all-terrain vehicles. We had positioned ourselves roughly 60 degrees off the target when we finally got clearance to go below the hard deck. As I remember, the call came that we "were cleared to prosecute as necessary".

'The terrain was very rugged around us, and I told my wingman to remain in high cover – MANPADS were our greatest threat. We armed the guns and left them hot until we were "Winchester" (out of ammunition). We made four full strafing runs, with the gun firing out on

Manned up and ready to go as part of the next launch cycle from the 'TR', crews in two VF-102 jets watch a bombless F/A-18C from VMFA-251 return to CVN-71 at the end of yet another Afghanistan mission on 15 November 2001. The 'Diamond-backs' struck up a solid working relationship with the 'Thunderbolts' in OEF, as VF-102's maintenance officer recalled. 'The Marine Corps pilots tended to be more CAS savvy due to the emphasis they placed on supporting their brethren on the ground during training. VMFA-251 also fitted AN/ASQ-173 laser spot trackers to all their jets as a matter of course, rather than as an optional extra. This store proved greatly beneficial to the Hornet pilot when he buddy-lased LGBs or LMAVs with a LANTIRN-equipped Tomcat, as the LST allowed him to pick out laser energy from the F-14's targeting pod' (*US Navy*)

the fifth. We set the radar altimeter for 2500 ft MSL so that we would level out by 2000 ft MSL.

'I made sure that we entered each strafing run with a speed of more than 540 knots over the nose of the jet, with most of our run-ins being made along the same approach line. You could see the SAFHEI rounds exploding on impact, and the flashes of small arms fire shot back in our direction in return. We knew that we were out of their range, but we never discounted the "golden BB" rule. It would have only taken one round to ruin our day.

Gunpowder residue stains the cannon muzzle blast fairing on 'Blacklion 101' following its strafing mission on 5 November 2001. With the Tomcat's General Electric M61A1 Vulcan 20 mm cannon firing at a rate of 6000 rounds per minute, the weapon's magazine (into which 678 rounds could be loaded) would take just 8.8 seconds to empty (*Cdr Chip King*)

Cdr Chip King (left) and Lt Cdr Kevin Claffy compare notes on the flightdeck at the end of an OEF mission in early November 2001. Behind them, one of VF-213's hard-working armourer teams has already started uploading GBU-12s onto the jet's belly pallet rails (*Lt Tony Toma*)

'I remember thinking to myself at the time what a disparity in technology. It was like "Buck Rogers" meeting the "Arabian Nights", with the Taleban fighters on horseback. Our fire was effective, allowing Northern Alliance forces to retreat without suffering further casualties.

'Once we were "Winchester", we stayed overhead until "Tiger" called "Clear". He was very grateful, and thanked us, saying that he looked forward to buying us a beer upon our return home. By then Lt Cdr Peterson and our wingman were coordinating relief with new strike assets that had been vectored to the fight as we made our way to the tanker.

'Word of our strafing runs had not yet reached CVN-70's flightdeck by the time we recovered. I remember seeing my "Gunner's" eyes, and the excitement of the folks "on the roof", as we turned out of the landing area. The jet's side was covered in gunpowder residue, and I wasn't sure if they would ever clean it off! This was the first time the F-14's gun had been used in an air-to-ground role, and the first use of 20 mm SAFHEI in OEF.'

The battle for control of Mazar-e-Sharif continued the following day, and again VF-213 found itself in the thick of the action south of the city.

Lt Geoff Vickers and Lt(jg) Tony Toma were flying as wing during a FAC(A) mission. Despite their aircraft ('Blacklion 111') suffering from systems failures that manifested themselves after launching – MFD 2 in the front cockpit and MFD 3 in the rear cockpit were inoperable, and the pilot's MFD 1 could not view LTS imagery – the crew pressed on.

According to RIO Lt(jg) Toma, 'these failures would make our LGB deliveries extremely difficult, as I had to drive the pilot into release parameters, while trying to simultaneously shield the TID (the F-14Ds were the last Tomcats to get the improved PTID) from the sun and work the LTS. Lt Vickers had to trust me that our delivery was both valid and on the appropriate target.

'Upon checking in with "Bossman", we were informed that the Northern Alliance had just overrun a small town approximately 100 nautical miles south of Mazar-e-Sharif. Our FAC, "Tiger 2A", was requesting our immediate assistance in targeting and destroying vehicles that were evacuating Taleban forces from the town to the north and west. All vehicles moving in this area were declared hostile, as all friendly forces were either on foot or on horseback. "Tiger 2A" stated that the vehicles were aware of our presence, and were attempting to hide.

'Our Tomcat lead acquired a car travelling west and successfully delivered a bomb that destroyed it. We then had to proceed to our fragged tanker due to us reaching a low fuel state. We assured "Tiger 2A" that we would return, and 20 minutes later we were back on station. Our lead prosecuted three more vehicles with his remaining bombs, although two of the LGBs did not guide – the third destroyed another car.

'The focus now shifted to vehicles attempting to flee on a valley road leading north to Mazar-e-Sharif. I still had my two bombs, and with the FAC(A)'s help, we were able to acquire two vehicles – a car followed by a large truck – moving rapidly to the north. I set up for a delivery on the lead vehicle, and the bomb directly impacted the car, while the blast destroyed the truck as well. All other vehicles along the road immediately attempted to hide, but I was able to acquire and deliver on another truck that had parked to the east of the road. The bomb was a direct hit, and the burning truck could still be seen well enough to be used as a mark for the section of "Blacklion" Tomcats that relieved us on station 15 minutes later.

'We later received a report passed via SOF assets that the trucks we hit burned for a long time because they were carrying ammunition that the Taleban was attempting to move to Mazar-e-Sharif.'

The fall of Mazar-e-Sharif on 9 November was the first in a series of victories achieved in a four-week period that would end Taleban control in Afghanistan. Kabul followed just four days later, and CVW-11's DCAG, Capt Chuck Wright, played his part in the capture of the Afghan capital when he helped Northern Alliance forces seize Bagram air base;

'Although I was a light strike guy (almost 4000 hours in TA-4s, A-7Es and F/A-18s) when I joined CVW-11, I quickly converted to the F-14D and built up my hours during work-ups. I felt so at home in the aircraft by early October 2001 that I chose to fly my first OEF combat mission in an F-14D. VF-213 was the most undermanned squadron in the air wing for pilots, so I didn't feel like I was stealing flight time from junior officers when I flew with the "Black Lions". I was essentially the unit's 14th pilot. The Hornet squadrons each had 17 pilots, in addition to an air wing staff pilot and a CAG and DCAG who were both F/A-18-qualified.

'VF-213 was scheduled in a similar way to each of the three Hornet units, flying ATO missions, as well as a fair share of the CAPs that were performed over the fleet. All four TACAIR squadrons in CVW-11 tallied 1000+ flight hours a month in October and November 2001, and were on track to do that again in December until we headed home on the 16th.

'By the time Kabul fell on 13 November, I had flown a handful of missions with VF-213, and dropped a fair number of the 15 LGBs that I would expend with the unit during the campaign.

'Upon checking in with "Bossman", my section was told to head to Bagram and work with a SOF FAC who was controlling jets that were providing CAS for the Northern Alliance push on the base. My RIO on this mission was CAG Ops officer Cdr Bob Proano, who I enjoyed flying with. We checked in with the FAC, who we thought was in the airfield's burned-out control tower – we never did find out his precise location.

'He asked us if we could see the runway – you couldn't miss it, as it was the dominant feature of the valley that Bagram was located in! He said that the runway length was one unit of measure, and to look that distance southwest of the southern end of it, where there was a bridge across a small river. We saw that. He said, "Anything moving south on that road, south of the bridge, is hostile". We rogered that and started looking south.

'The first thing that we saw was a burning tank along the road a few miles away. The smoke made a good reference point. South of that, the road went up and down some low ridges toward Kabul – then still in Taleban hands, but not for much longer. We spotted what looked liked a step-van heading south, so we offset to come at it head on. Hitting moving vehicles with an LGB is best done head-on, as it minimises the crossing rate and maximises the aerodynamic capability of the bombs as they approach the target. Bomb time-of-fall was roughly 45 seconds.

'Just after the first bomb was away, we saw a car go flying past the truck doing at least 80 mph. I got really excited and told my RIO to "follow the car, as anything going that fast had to be somebody important". He did a great job keeping the laser spot on the vehicle as it moved, the sedan reaching the top of one of the low hills that surrounded Kabul and then suddenly pulling off the road. The doors all flew open, and just as the occupants started to get out the 1000-lb LGB arrived.

'It turned out that the bad guys would drive really fast for a mile or two then get out and hide. If the car didn't blow up after a couple of minutes, they'd get back in and do it again. Our timing was better than theirs.

'In all the excitement of the car, we'd lost sight of the truck. We trolled up and down that road for a while until we found it hiding under a tree near a bridge abutment. Our other bomb took care of the truck, but the bad guys were probably safely under the bridge or in the gully hiding out.'

The fall of Kabul indicated to Gen Franks that OEF was proceeding precisely to plan, and he told the press on 15 November that 'we have said all along that it's all about condition-setting, followed by our attaining our objectives. The first thing we did was set conditions to begin to take down the tactical air defence. The next thing we did was to set conditions with these SOF teams, and the positioning of our aviation assets, to be able to take the Taleban apart or fracture it'.

That same day, VF-102 performed a series of post-dawn strikes west of Kandahar that would see two of its naval aviators subsequently awarded the Distinguished Flying Cross (DFC) for their exploits under fire. Two FAC(A)-qualified second-tour lieutenants played a pivotal role in the day's action, the pilot recalling;

'My RIO and I were leading a two-Tomcat section with the call-sign "Brando" flight, and we had launched from CVN-71 just before dawn. We headed north to relieve VF-102's "Segal" flight, which had been providing FAC(A) support for a three-man SEAL team 30 miles west of Kandahar. As they had neared the end of their vul time, "Segal" flight had been told by "Bossman" to check in with the team, which had just bedded down in a ravine so as to get some rest during the hours of daylight. They would be heading north after sunset, and they wanted the Tomcat section to check that their route was clear of any enemy activity.

'The SEALs had unfurled an orange tarpaulin to mark their position, and "Segal" flight soon had a visual tally on them. Just minutes after overflying their position, the lead Tomcat crew saw 10-15 tanks and APCs all laid out in perfect columns. They were just three miles from the SEALs, who were immediately asked by "Segal" flight lead if they were Northern Alliance assets – the VF-102 crews were concerned that they may have spotted Marine Corps M1 Abrams tanks, as Camp Rhino had recently been established not too far from here. The SEAL controller came back on the radio moments later and confirmed that these weren't friendly forces, telling the Tomcat crews to "take them out"!

'"Segal" flight quickly expended its LGBs, and also controlled four Hornets that were vectored in by "Bossman". Another division was also inbound, but the Tomcats were forced to leave the area prior to their arrival due to a shortage of fuel and ordnance. They provided us with a precise target turnover and then headed off home via the duty tanker.

'My RIO and I quickly conducted our own reconnaissance of the area, while our wingman circled overhead the SEALs and waited for additional air wing assets to come up with more ordnance – we did not want to drop our own GBU-12s (three per jet) just in case the guys that had been attacked packed up and started heading south towards the SOF team. If this did indeed happen prior to additional strike aircraft reaching us, we would have to take the enemy force out ourselves in real time.

'While holding at 15,000 ft in a $55 million aeroplane, we stumbled across yet more enemy vehicles using a $300 pair of gyro-stabilised Canon binoculars! These tanks, APCs and trucks were revetted and hidden beneath tents, with 13 vehicles in one location, 15-20 nearby and a third group of a similar size again in the same area. Over the next two-and-a-half hours (we ended up being extended for two cycles), with our wingman watching out for SAMs on our behalf, we controlled 18 sections of strike aircraft from CVW-1 as they pounded the crap out of the Taleban vehicles and tanks.

'We lased for a good number of the Hornet crews who attacked these targets. With some of the more senior strike-fighter guys in the air wing, we offered them our lasing expertise after they checked in, but all they required were target coordinates and they would then go and take them out. With junior crews, who were struggling to work the Hornet's notoriously difficult NITE Hawk targeting pod, they were more than happy – indeed, they were relieved – to take us up on

A pilot from VF-102 makes a final check on the GBU-16s shackled to the forward belly pallets of his jet during his mandatory preflight walkaround. The red-shirted 'ordie' beneath the LGB is making some final last-minute adjustments to the bomb's all-important guidance unit. 'VF-102 dropped 680 LGBs in OEF, and we only had five duds', recalled the unit's gunner, CWO3 Carleton Roe. 'Three were due to failures in the AN/AWW-4 Fuze Function Control Set box fitted in the F-14, which meant that the bombs were dropped without being armed'. Fellow gunner CWO3 Michael Lavoie of VF-213 explained to the Author just how difficult it was to attach bombs to the Tomcat;

'All ordnance had to be physically lifted onto the pallet rails, as we could not fit a SHOLS (single hoist ordnance loading system) beneath the jet. For all LGBs, including the large GBU-10s, -16s and -24s, you could lower the rail and attach the weapon to it, before winching it back up flush in the weapons pallet. We could have lifted 500-lb GBU-12s, as we did with dumb Mk 83s, but by lowering the rail to the weapon, we avoided accidentally damaging the bomb sensor during manual loading' (*US Navy*)

The large 8 x 8-inch PTID screen in the rear cockpit of a VF-102 F-14B reveals the rugged Afghan landscape near Tarin Kowt on 17 November 2001. This view, obtained via the LTS pod while circling the target area at 31,980 ft, could be panned in or out, depending on the mission requirements. No other TACAIR platform in OEF – Navy or Air Force – had a tactical display of this size, and when combined with the LTS pod, the Tomcat became the precision bomber and SCAR/FAC(A) platform of choice in-theatre (*VF-102*)

'Before' and 'after' shots of two Taleban T-62M Main Battle Tanks, caught out in the open by a TARPS-equipped VF-213 jet on 11 November 2001. These photographs were taken by the pod's KS-153B camera, the tanks having been struck by GBU-12s (*VF-213*)

our offer to lase targets for them. They simply asked us for the coordinates that we wanted them to drop on so that they could place their LGB in the LTS's laser basket, and we would handle it from there. Our wingman's FLIR was down on this mission too, so we lased his three bombs as well.

'As we neared the end of our second cycle, we asked for a third trip to the tanker so as to extend our time on station, but "Bossman" told us that our relief was inbound to take over from us. By then we had just one GBU-12 left on our jet, but there were still targets that had not yet been attacked. We had kept our eye on a large vehicle parked in the corner of a revetment near to what we thought might be a temporary fuel depot. My RIO shacked the target with the LGB, and as we were coming off the bombing run, I peered through my binoculars and saw dozens of enemy troops fleeing for their lives from the revetment that we had just hit.

'On the way back to the boat, we were on the tanker when my RIO was asked by "Bossman" if we had sufficient gas to perform a supersonic low-level pass for a nearby SOF team? They were trying to infuse a little muscle into stalled negotiations with stubborn local tribal chiefs who were proving reluctant to help them fight the Taleban. As Tomcat guys, we were always keen to show the jet off, and such a flyby would have been a perfect opportunity for us to do just that. Frustratingly, we could not get our deck recovery time extended back at the boat, so we were unable to fulfil this request – my RIO and I bitched about this all the way home.'

TARIN KOWT

On 17 November, with Northern Alliance forces now heading south towards the Taleban heartland around Kandahar, VF-102's maintenance officer and his RIO were involved in one of the most memorable Tomcat actions of OEF. The former detailed the mission to the Author;

'We had just finished tanking, and were on our way up to Kunduz to help support the Northern Alliance, when two Marine Hornet pilots from VMFA-251 got on the radio to the AWACS and said that they had spotted a convoy of 40+ Taleban vehicles heading north to Tarin Kowt, capital of Uruzgan province. The residents of this town (recognised by most Afghans as being at the heart of the Taleban movement) had ejected a small Taleban force from the area just hours earlier. We quickly realised that the convoy was only 40 miles away from us, so we turned our section around and headed back south prior to "Bossman" telling us to do so – we knew that there was a lot going on there.'

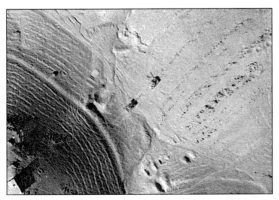

Hours earlier, Pashtun leader, and future Afghan president, Hamid Karzai had sent word to his supporters in Tarin Kowt to start a revolt, and once this was underway, he and his small force of Afghan fighters had moved in – 11 members of SOF A-Team 574 had accompanied Karzai into the town. Taleban forces in Kandahar were soon alerted to the fall of Tarin Kowt, and they were hell bent on retaking the town.

'As we raced towards Tarin Kowt, my RIO managed to get onto the frequency that was being used by one of the combat controllers who had the enemy convoy in his sights as it neared the town', explained the VF-102 pilot. 'He told us that there were vehicles on the move up the valley that led to a mountain pass two miles from Tarin Kowt. The controller wanted to know if we could see the road that the enemy force was driving along. The Marine jets had already left the scene due to a shortage of fuel, but they had hit the convoy with their GBU-12s prior to departing. Despite thermal crossover problems besetting their NITE Hawk pods – the pilots had attacked at dawn – they had destroyed one vehicle and disabled another. The smoke rising from the burning pick-ups clearly marked the convoy's position for us south of Tarin Kowt.

'The vehicles had been hit near a bridge at the entrance to the bowl-like valley, and by the time we reached the target area, they had moved much closer to the mountain pass that led directly to the town. Despite having taken losses, the Taleban had pressed on regardless. This was the first time that we had seen this kind of determination by the enemy to reach their objective. When we checked in, I started panicking because I knew that as soon as the Taleban got into the town, we would not be able to attack them due to their proximity to friendly forces and civilians.

'The controller on the ground then told us that his squad was heading back to the town from their scouting position on a rocky outcrop overlooking the valley. The Northern Alliance fighters with the A-Team had basically piled back into their vehicles upon seeing the size of the Taleban force heading their way, and the SOF troops could not convince them that air power would deal with the threat! They too had had to head back to Tarin Kowt, as they had no other form of transport with which to evacuate the area should things have become too hot on the ground.

'By the time we spotted the convoy, enemy forces were heading for the town in military trucks, rather than civilian-type pick-ups. As a FAC(A) crew, we immediately took control of the TACAIR aspect of the defence of Tarin Kowt. The first thing we did was to detach our wingman and tell him that his target was the northernmost truck. We then set ourselves up as "goalie" just in case they couldn't hit it. We needn't have worried, because the XO and his pilot did a superb job of stopping the truck with a direct hit, despite their LGB dudding. We hit another vehicle and the convoy ground to a halt, at which point Taleban fighters started to spread out into the valley on foot.

'Moments later the combat controller requested that we check the other road passes that led into Tarin Kowt to make sure that no one was approaching the town from another direction, and to confirm that the A-Team also had a clear escape route. Our wingman detached and started to scour the area, while we continued to work over targets in the valley.

'By now "Bossman" had figured out that more assets were needed to stop the Taleban advance, and additional jets were vectored in from

CVW-1. We ended up handling six sections of Hornets and Tomcats, and the AWACS even moved the duty tanker closer to us so that we had less distance to fly when it came time to refuel. We provided more than 30 controls for jets dropping LGBs and Mk 83 airburst bombs (the latter from F-14s), and expended 20 mm SAFHEI rounds in three runs.

'The cannon was our weapon of last resort, as we had run out of ordnance and there was no one available to relieve us on station. We really didn't want to strafe, but we had no choice, as the nearest jet with bombs was still more than ten minutes away. We had been forced to use all our LGBs in the early stages of the engagement when the Taleban threatened to overrun Tarin Kowt. The next two sections of CVW-1 strikers on station also did some great work, with their weapons being skilfully buddy-lased by my RIO against some rapidly moving targets.

'By then our wingman was also out of bombs, and with no other assets close by, there was a lull in our attacks on the Taleban positions. Sensing their opportunity, a handful of troops got back into their vehicles, and a solitary tank, and made a dash for Tarin Kowt, forcing us to make strafing runs on them. Despite the main valley pass being blocked, enemy troops kept on remounting and taking to the scrub in an effort to get around the destroyed trucks. The vehicles were full of fighters, who would quickly get out when they heard jet noise. Bombs would then destroy a vehicle or two, and as the jet noise decreased, the Taleban would emerge from the scrub, board the surviving trucks and drive another quarter-mile until the next bombing pass was made. Then the whole routine was repeated again. They were determined to get to Tarin Kowt.

'Having spoken about strafing within the unit during our work-ups, we had agreed that the gun would only be used as a weapon of last resort in a danger close situation. With the tank clearly on the move, we went for a classical forward quarter attack. My wingman strafed first, and his gun jammed after he had fired just one burst. We then came in from the same direction and made two passes, and although I am uncertain as to whether we hit the tank or not, it stopped and a crewman got out. A third pass was made on a moving half-ton truck, and it too was stopped in its tracks.

'The ground controller was happy to let us handle the TACAIR assets throughout this engagement once he realised that we had the training and experience to ensure that our bombs would indeed hit their intended targets. Aside from the strafing runs, we only had one other danger close call during the sortie when we spotted dust being kicked up on the edge of town. Thinking that we had somehow let a vehicle slip through the net, it turned out that the dust was being created by dudes on donkeys!'

Both the maintenance officer and his RIO received DFCs for their efforts during the course of this mission.

Sadly, not all danger close actions met with this level of success, as was the case on 26 November when Taleban and al-Qaeda fighters that were captured following the fall of Mazar-e-Sharif rioted in the nearby Qala-i-Janghi fortress, which was being used as a prison. CIA agent Johnny Spann was killed during the uprising and the fortress' armoury seized. Air power was quickly called in by US 10th Mountain Division troops and a team from the British SAS as they fought alongside the Northern Alliance in the close confines of the ancient fortress. VF-102's maintenance officer and his RIO were flying the second jet to arrive on the scene.

'My pilot and I happened to be running TARPS missions in northern Afghanistan when "Bossman" called us in as the riot escalated', recalled the first-cruise RIO. 'We had no idea just how bad the situation in the prison was, as "Bossman" simply told us midway through our TARPS run that he needed us to go to Mazar-e-Sharif and talk to a SOF JTAC. We switched up the radio to the frequency that we had been given and began listening to what was occurring on the ground. Three minutes ahead of us were two Hornets from VMFA-251, and they were the first TACAIR assets to arrive on the scene. We could hear that there was confusion between the SOF forces on the ground and the guys in the air.

'I wrote the JDAM coordinates down that were given to the lead Hornet pilot as the target for his bomb, as well as the position of the friendly troops, and quickly typed them into the mission computer. My pilot immediately asked me how far apart the friendly and enemy positions were, and I replied that they were too close to tell – there was less than 300 metres' separation between the coordinates. Unfortunately, the latter were passed the wrong way around to the pilot in the confusion, and his 2000-lb GBU-31 JDAM went precisely where it was directed, killing six Northern Alliance fighters and wounding five American troops.

'The radios went deathly quiet after the JDAM hit the ground, and the firing that we had seen from both sides of the compound stopped. The Hornet pilot tried to raise the SOF Texas team on the ground, but there was no response. This was not a good sign. About 90 seconds later a voice came on the radio and shouted "Check Fire, Check Fire, Check Fire!" We knew then that the weapon had hit the wrong target.

'There was not a cloud in the sky that day, and the riot in the fortress would have been an ideal target scenario for an LGB attack, as we could have had a talk-on to the target area by the JTAC. This would have drastically reduced the chances of us bombing our own troops, as you aim your LGB at what you are looking at through the FLIR. You cannot do a target talk-on with a JDAM. Instead, you have to hope that the target coordinates passed to you by the JTAC are correct.

'We conducted our photo runs over the fortress down to 15,000 ft, but we never got any lower than that because of the MANPAD threat. Aside from the photos, we also wrote down plenty of notes while circling the fortress so that we could help CVW-1 with the post-mission debrief.'

Such incidents did not stop the inexorable advance of the Northern Alliance southward to Kandahar, the spiritual home of the Taleban. It was also the enemy's last stronghold by the beginning of December. Also heading for the city from the south was Hamid Karzai's Pashtun force, again with SOF teams in support. In response to stiff opposition encountered on the ground, 90 TACAIR sorties were flown by CTF-50 carriers on 1 December alone – USAF strike aircraft and heavy bombers flew an additional 44 sorties. In the face of this overwhelming air power, all resistance in the city collapsed on 4 December and surviving enemy fighters fled into the mountains northeast of the city.

TORA BORA

With the fall of Kandahar signalling an end to the Taleban's political control of Afghanistan, CENTCOM shifted its attention to seeking out the remnants of al-Qaeda in the rugged Tora Bora region of the country

Below Right
VF-102's colour jet heads for Tora Bora in early December 2001. Note that the aircraft carries a mixed load of GBU-12s and Mk 83 TDD-fused dumb bombs. 'We were forced to drop a quantity of LGBs in the sea aft of the ship at the end of some of the missions flown in early December, when we could not find targets to bomb', recalled a pilot from the 'Diamondbacks'. 'Still typically launching with four GBU-12s, as we had been during the previous big months of October and November, once things got quiet following the fall of Kandahar, we were now having to jettison two of them in order to make our minimum landing weight before trapping back aboard the carrier.

'It was decided that we should start flying with mixed loads that included dumb bombs on the rear pallets, as it would be much cheaper to jettison these instead of two LGBs. Once the Tora Bora offensive commenced, we no longer had to worry about bomb bring back, but we stuck with the mixed loads nevertheless. I got to drop four or five dumb bombs, including two on troops disembarking from trucks that we were called in to strike in the far north of the country – we had already dropped our GBU-12s by the time we were sent up there.

'During the course of this particular mission, I recalled a discussion I had had with my fellow students when going through the bombing phase of my F-14 pilot's course at VF-101 some years earlier. I was adamant that the Navy was never going to let a Tomcat, with its old weapon delivery system, drop dumb bombs in combat! Yet here I was four years later doing just that.

'The dumb bombs were delivered from an angle of 45 degrees, rolling the jet into the target and making sure that the latter was about the right distance away when I pickled the ordnance. The 500-lb Mk 82s and 1000-lb Mk 83s were fine to use against a large target such as vehicles or troops in the open, where you weren't trying to sling the bomb through the front door of a building. Most of the 50 dumb bombs that we dropped were delivered during the day, as it was difficult to accurately acquire targets for the weapon at night' (*VF-102*) near the central eastern border with Pakistan. Again, carrier air power would play a key role in this offensive, SOF and CIA teams coordinating air strikes during the campaign, which ran from 10 to 19 December.

Almost at the end of its OEF tour of duty, CVW-11 played only a minor role in the preparatory stages of the Tora Bora operation. VF-213 flew a handful of XCAS missions supporting Coalition troops as they entered the Spinghar mountain range surrounding Tora Bora, Lt Kris Gasko and Lt(jg) Tony Toma seeing action on the night of 7 December.

'My lead for the event called that their jet was down because of an LTS failure, so we launched and waited at "Shamrock" for the spare, which filled for them', explained Lt(jg) Toma. 'The spare's LTS pod wasn't working either, so I knew that I would have to find and lase any targets. We checked in with "K-Mart" (AWACS) and were told to head to Tora Bora to work with "Cobra 25", who had arrived in the area that very day.

'Intel had been receiving good information placing Osama Bin Laden in the locale, but the mountains were heavily defended.

'"Cobra 25" was working one side of a ridgeline while "VB 02" – a Delta Force FAC – worked the other side. A Hornet section from VFA-22 checked in with "Cobra 25" just prior to us, but they were not able to drop because they were carrying JDAM and GBU-12s, but no FLIR pod. They had brought an LST (laser spot tracker), but the ground FAC did not have a laser that was capable of picking out targets. "K-Mart" would not authorise JDAM release because there were too many friendlies in the area, and they did not trust the coordinates given by the inexperienced FACs. A B-1B was also attempting to work the target area, but it wasn't allowed to release its JDAM either.

'We checked in and informed "Cobra 25" that we were both FLIR- and laser-capable, so he began a visual talk-on – augmented by "Sparkling" with his handheld infrared pointer – so that we could acquire the target through our NVGs. "Cobra" concurrently cleared the B-1 to set up for a Mk 84 dumb bomb delivery. The Hornets left to refuel and we began alternating delivery runs with the B-1 on al-Qaeda fighters that had dug themselves in on a ridgeline above the friendly position.

'I delivered my three GBU-12s and then lased for my wingman's two LGBs. All bombs guided accurately and went high order. "Cobra" called "good hits", and had us walking each bomb 200 metres south along the ridgeline until we were "Winchester". It was impossible to tell how many troops were killed, but the FAC reported that enemy fire in his area had ceased. As we headed away from Tora Bora in search of our tanker, the Hornets returned and requested that we lase their bombs for them. I would have been happy to, but we had already stayed too long and our fuel state was getting dangerously low. We returned home, and were the only Navy assets to drop ordnance that day.'

CVN-71/CVW-11 left the Northern Arabian Sea and headed home nine days later, by which point VF-213 had expended 435,000 lbs of laser-guided ordnance and flown 500+ sorties (totalling 2600 combat flight hours) during its ten weeks in OEF.

The *Carl Vinson* battle group had been relieved by USS *John C Stennis* (CVN-74) and CVW-9 on 15 December, the latter having left San Diego two months ahead of its original schedule on 12 November. With CVN-74 being designated the night carrier, CVW-9's TACAIR units saw limited action during the final 48 hours of the Tora Bora offensive. The bulk of the naval air power committed to this operation was provided by CVW-1, with VF-102 seeing particularly heavy mission tasking. The unit's maintenance officer summed up the 'Diamondbacks'' campaign as follows;

'The Tora Bora sorties proved challenging for us, as we were essentially trying to hit little more than a rock blocking a cave entrance in very rugged terrain at high altitude right on the Afghan-Pakistan border. The close proximity of the latter meant that we could not spill out into Pakistani airspace after making our bombing runs.

'Breaking out the key rock that needed to be bombed through the FLIR when it was the same colour as its surroundings proved a virtually impossible task. Things became even worse at night, as at least during the day you could talk to your RIO and the ground controller about what they were seeing. The location of the troops on the ground was not ideal either, as they tended to be further away from the cave entrances that needed bombing than we would have liked – this was particularly the case at night. Occasionally, you would see enemy troops moving in the Tora Bora area, and the LTS also picked up hotpots of activity.'

During the early hours of 12 December, Coalition troops were engaged by large numbers of al-Qaeda and Taleban fighters holed up in cave complexes in the Tora Bora area. Heavily outnumbered, the SOF teams again relied on air support from VF-102 and other CENTAF assets

The pilots and NFOs of VF-213 get together with 'Blacklion 101' and a selection of LGBs (from left to right, a GBU-16, GBU-24 and GBU-10) towards the end of the unit's OEF cruise. Boasting a 99.6 percent sortie-completion rate during its ten-week spell in the Northern Arabian Sea, VF-213 expended 452 bombs and 470 20 mm cannon rounds on cruise. Of the ordnance dropped by the unit, only eight Mk 83 bombs and two Mk 99 CBUs were non-precision guided munitions. The 'Black Lions' were credited with expending four GBU-24s, ten GBU-10s, 157 GBU-16s and a whopping 271 GBU-12s. By comparison, in OIF in 2003, the unit dropped just 102 LGBs and 94 JDAM due to its operations in northern Iraq being badly affected by poor weather (*VF-213*)

With its rattlesnake suitably adorned with a Christmas hat, 'Diamondback 115' (BuNo 161608) joins the landing pattern on 19 December 2001 – the Tora Bora offensive ended that very day. 'We all found Tora Bora a challenge simply because we often didn't know exactly what, or who, we were bombing', recalled VF-102's operations officer. 'There was also a lot more interest shown in what we were doing by the higher ups in Washington, D.C. than had previously been the case.

'It was nerve-wracking dropping ordnance on targets that you could not positively identify before pickling your bomb. FACs could mark the target with hand-held infrared pointers or a smoke round from a mortar, but there was nothing to break that spot out as being an obvious target to us while we circled at 20,000 ft.

'I was unsure about just how effective we had been during this offensive until several months after Tora Bora, when a huge warrant officer SEAL strode into our ready room and demanded to see me. I stood up and asked him what he wanted. "Sir, I just wanted you to know that we were conducting a patrol in Tora Bora when you helped us out after we had come under heavy fire. I got your name from the CAG, as I wanted to give you these". He handed me a small bottle that was filled with Afghan sand and an optical sight that he had broken off an SA-7 shoulder-launched SAM. "Thanks for saving our arses Sir". He then left the ready room' (*VF-102*)

to counter the threat posed by the enemy. The unit's training officer became embroiled in the action, as he explained to the Author;

'As was often the case in night missions during the Tora Bora campaign, we had an AC-130 gunship mark the cave entrances for us. My female RIO and I could not break out the targets that we were supposed to be bombing even with the LTS, so the "Spooky" crew used their humungous suite of targeting sensors at a considerably lower altitude than us to pick out the cave entrances amongst the rocks in the area. When we asked them to mark the target for us, they fired "Willie Pete" unguided rockets directly at the cave entrances that needed to be bombed. They were flying with all their lights off, which meant that we could not see them, so I had to wait for the pilot to tell us that they were five miles from the target before we went in and dropped our LGB.

'The bomb hit the cave and exploded, and moments later the hill literally erupted like an ant's nest, as people started scurrying away in all directions – we could clearly see them through the FLIR. If these guys were willing to expose themselves while an AC-130 and two Tomcats were circling overhead, then they were clearly either Taleban or al-Qaeda.

'I then made a call that I never thought I would have the chance to do – it was a call you made over the radio during CAS/FAC(A) training as a joke. "99. We've got troops on the move. Pass your laser codes and let's hit them". We handled section after section of Hornets that arrived overhead the target area in response to our call, lasing their LGBs as we attempted to hit as many of the enemy troops as we could before they escaped into the mountains.'

CVW-1's Hornets were kept busy throughout the Tora Bora offensive dropping 2000-lb GBU-31 JDAM fitted with J109 penetrator warheads in anti-cave missions. These weapons would bury themselves in several feet of rock prior to exploding. With VF-102's F-14Bs unable to employ JDAM (CVW-7, which would relieve CVW-1 in March 2002, had the first JDAM-capable Tomcats to reach the fleet), the unit instead focused on engaging enemy troops that had broken cover and were in the open once their caves had been bombed by the F/A-18s. VF-102 dropped a lot of 1000-lb Mk 83 TDD (Target Detector Device) general purpose bombs during this period, these weapons being fitted with air-burst fuses so as to maximise their effect against troops in the open.

USS *John C Stennis* (CVN-74) turns into wind as it prepares to launch one of the last strike missions sent to Tora Bora. VF-211 pilot Lt Dan Buchar explained to the Author how his unit prepared for OEF. 'We got dialled into the admin issues relating to operations in OEF by monitoring reports being uploaded onto the secure SIPR Net as we headed west. This allowed us to work out how best to get through Pakistan, how to find our tankers, what fuel numbers worked and what were the best bomb loadouts, all in advance of us arriving on station. The carriers involved in OEF before us did this leg work, and then dumped the information onto us when we checked in.

'We also got a face-to-face handover from key personnel in VF-102. They really emphasised the length of the missions that we were destined to fly, telling us to be prepared for six-hour missions. This would be different from anything that we had previously experienced, and would see us tank at least three times during a single mission, before landing at night. The admin aspects of these flights were also explained in detail, with an emphasis placed on making sure that you knew where your tankers were supposed to be before you left the ship. You had to stay ahead of the game when it came to making sure you had sufficient fuel, as their were few divert airfields.

'VF-102 also told us to be wary of MANPADS and AAA that had been moved up into the mountains to increase their range. Working with SOF was also touched upon, and how they varied in their abilities when it came to handling TACAIR. We were told that the "by the book" training terminology had been replaced by plain English in OEF, with SOF FACs simply getting on the radio and saying "Hey, we need a bomb here"' (*US Navy*)

As previously mentioned, CVN-74 and CVW-9 arrived in-theatre on 15 December 2001, and 36 hours later, VF-211 led the air wing's first strike. Unit operations officer, and RIO, Lt Cdr Nick Dienna, participated in these early missions in the last days of the Tora Bora campaign;

'I flew almost exclusively with our CO, Cdr Owen Honors, and we got to drop a small amount of ordnance early on. The weather had turned pretty bad by the time we reached the Northern Arabian Sea, and few aircraft got their bombs off during this early phase of the cruise. We saw a little bit of action in the last 48 hours of the Tora Bora operation, but after that we primarily flew on-call XCAS missions in sections and divisions, and it was really hit or miss as to whether you would end up bombing a target or not. Even in Tora Bora, that was predominantly a JDAM-only deal, which meant that the bulk of the ordnance was dropped by the three Hornet units in CVW-9.

'We continued to see very little action for the next two months up to the commencement of Operation *Anaconda* in early March. During a typical 12-hour flying day, out of the six sections of jets VF-211 would send up to Afghanistan, only one would usually get ordnance off – at most eight bombs, but more typically one or two per jet. We could individually expect to drop ordnance maybe once a week at most on average during the five months that we were committed to OEF. Our biggest problem during this slow period was fighting off complacency amongst the aircrew, as you did not want to be caught unprepared should you actually be called on to support troops in contact with the enemy.

'We often worked with Australian and British SAS patrols during this period as they went about clearing villages and towns of the last remnants of Taleban and al-Qaeda fighters. Typically, we would circle overhead and keep track of their progress through our LTS, remaining on call to support them with bombs should the need arise. I personally did not have to resort to dropping ordnance during any of these missions.'

The success of the Tora Bora campaign proved difficult to quantify, with Gen Franks later commenting that 'the pounding we put into that area, and the number of caves and compound complexes that were closed, made it virtually impossible to know how many fighters were killed'. Navy jets had dropped 2100 tons of bombs on the Tora Bora region by the end of the offensive, which was a staggering 25 percent of the total ordnance expended by TACAIR assets in OEF. Nevertheless, a large number of Taleban and al-Qaeda fighters escaped the net by slipping across the nearby border into Pakistan.

Once operations in the Tora Bora region had come to an end on 19 December, mission tasking changed for CTF-50. Instead of dropping bombs virtually every time they went in-country, TACAIR assets were now providing on-call XCAS for the increasing number of Coalition troops in Afghanistan. This effectively meant that VF-102 and VF-211 would not see much in the way of real action until the commencement of the shambolic Operation *Anaconda* offensive in early March 2002.

COLOUR PLATES

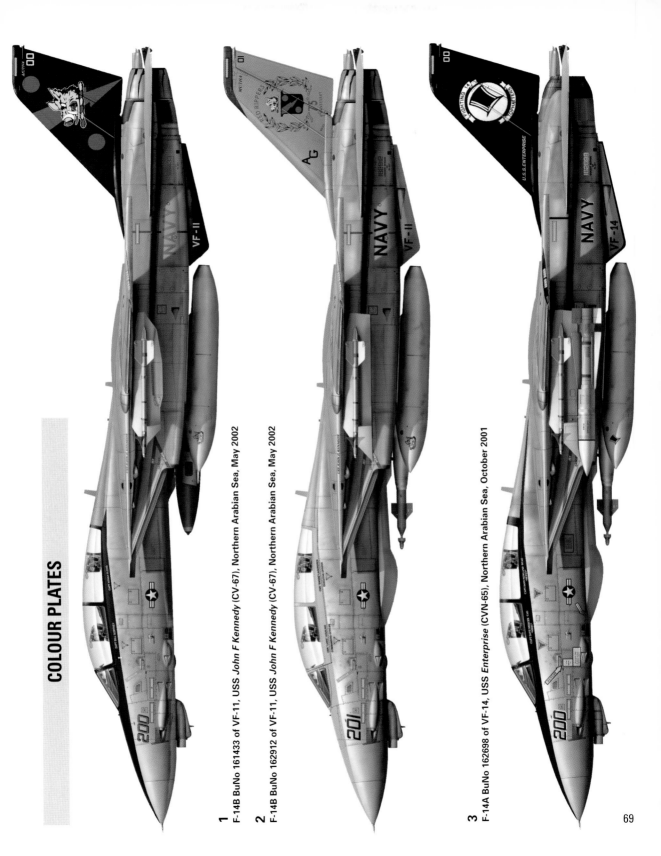

1
F-14B BuNo 161433 of VF-11, USS *John F Kennedy* (CV-67), Northern Arabian Sea, May 2002

2
F-14B BuNo 162912 of VF-11, USS *John F Kennedy* (CV-67), Northern Arabian Sea, May 2002

3
F-14A BuNo 162698 of VF-14, USS *Enterprise* (CVN-65), Northern Arabian Sea, October 2001

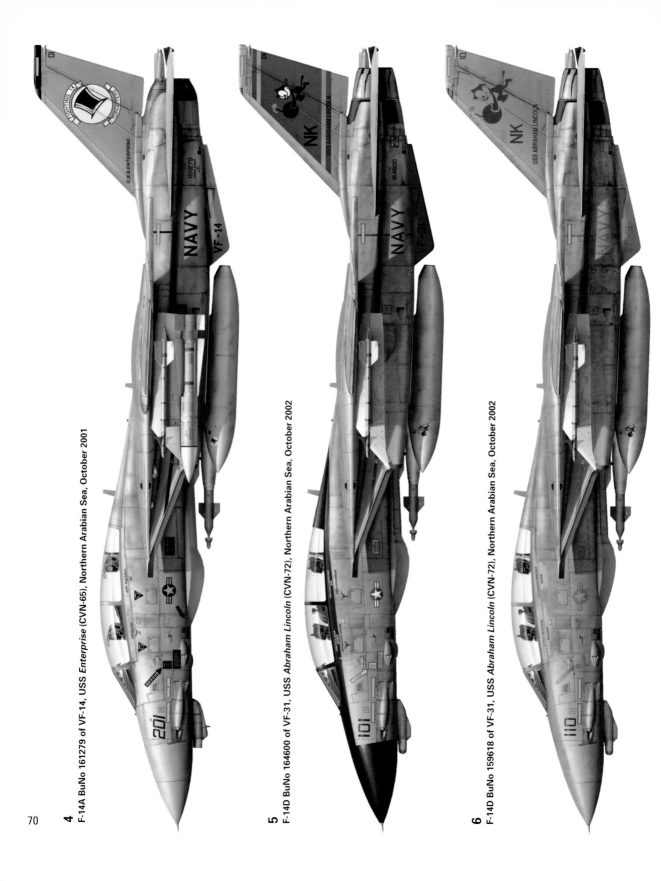

70

4
F-14A BuNo 161279 of VF-14, USS *Enterprise* (CVN-65), Northern Arabian Sea, October 2001

5
F-14D BuNo 164600 of VF-31, USS *Abraham Lincoln* (CVN-72), Northern Arabian Sea, October 2002

6
F-14D BuNo 159618 of VF-31, USS *Abraham Lincoln* (CVN-72), Northern Arabian Sea, October 2002

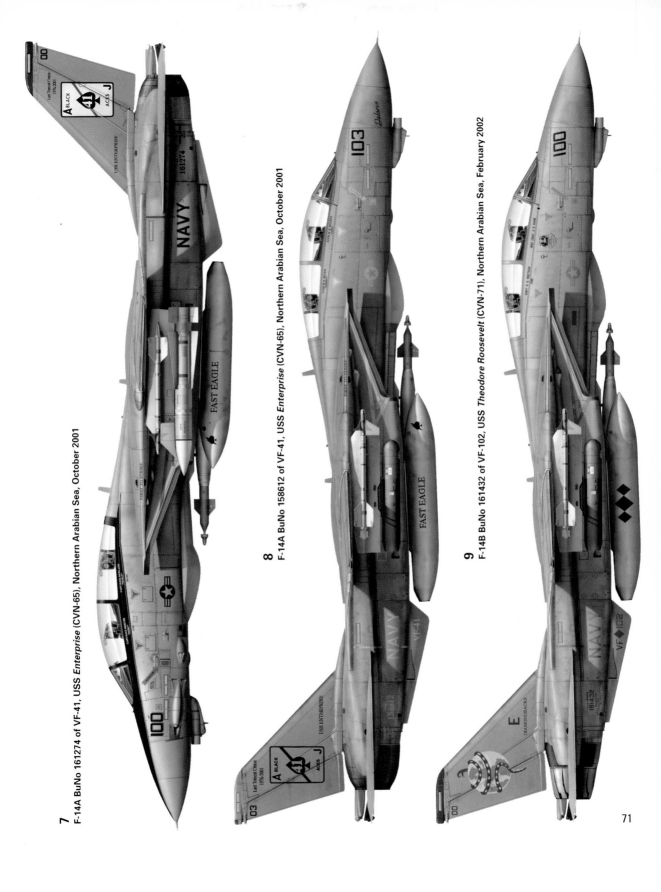

7
F-14A BuNo 161274 of VF-41, USS *Enterprise* (CVN-65), Northern Arabian Sea, October 2001

8
F-14A BuNo 158612 of VF-41, USS *Enterprise* (CVN-65), Northern Arabian Sea, October 2001

9
F-14B BuNo 161432 of VF-102, USS *Theodore Roosevelt* (CVN-71), Northern Arabian Sea, February 2002

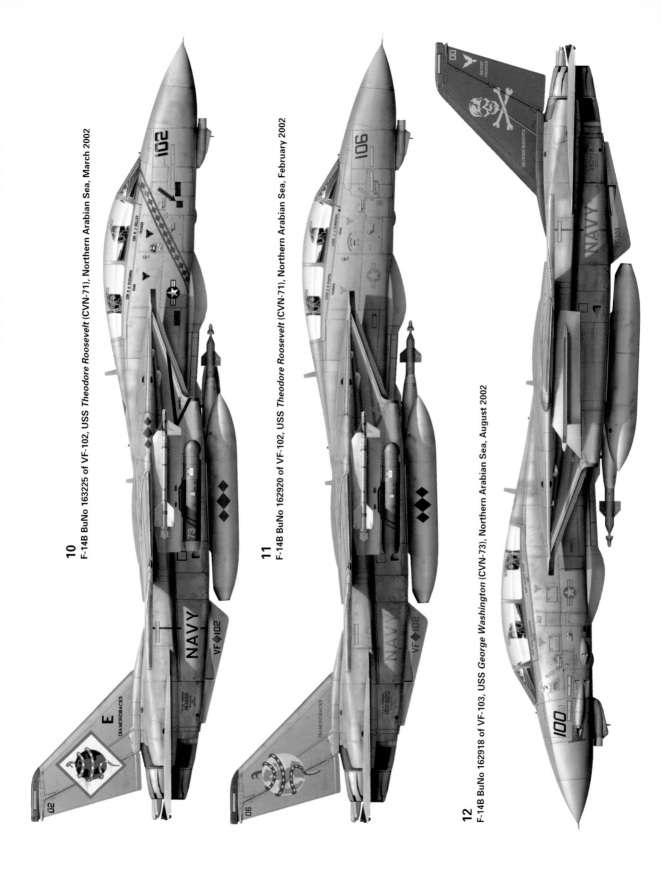

10
F-14B BuNo 163225 of VF-102, USS *Theodore Roosevelt* (CVN-71), Northern Arabian Sea, March 2002

11
F-14B BuNo 162920 of VF-102, USS *Theodore Roosevelt* (CVN-71), Northern Arabian Sea, February 2002

12
F-14B BuNo 162918 of VF-103, USS *George Washington* (CVN-73), Northern Arabian Sea, August 2002

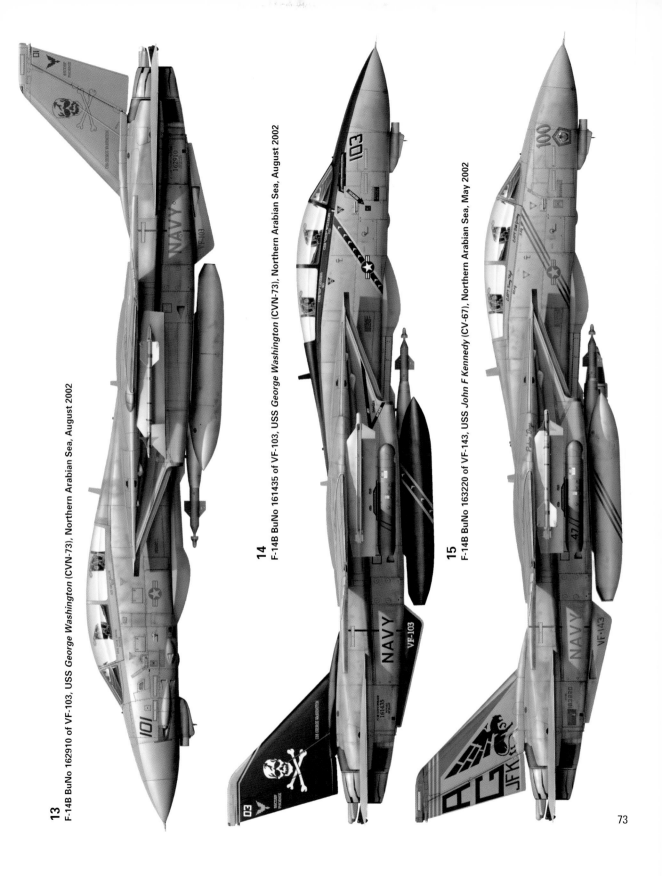

13
F-14B BuNo 162910 of VF-103, USS *George Washington* (CVN-73), Northern Arabian Sea, August 2002

14
F-14B BuNo 161435 of VF-103, USS *George Washington* (CVN-73), Northern Arabian Sea, August 2002

15
F-14B BuNo 163220 of VF-143, USS *John F Kennedy* (CV-67), Northern Arabian Sea, May 2002

73

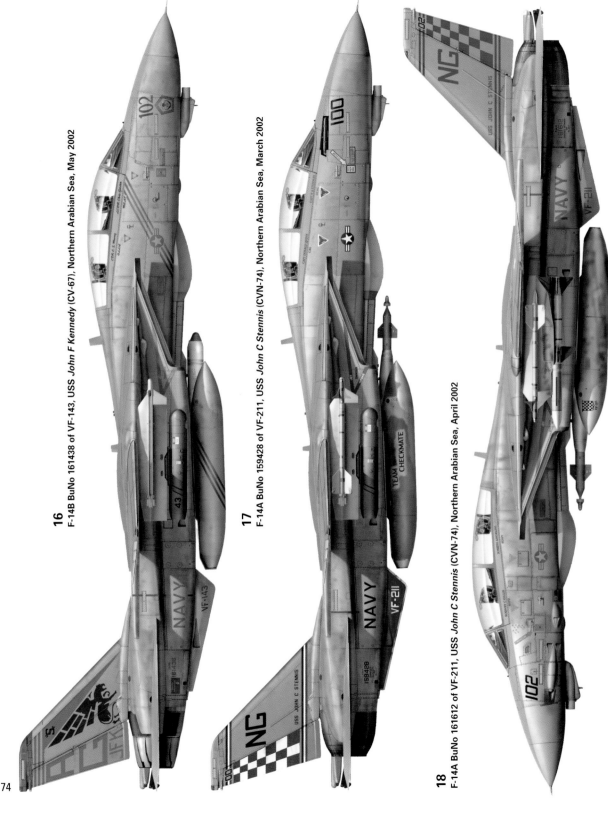

16
F-14B BuNo 161438 of VF-143, USS *John F Kennedy* (CV-67), Northern Arabian Sea, May 2002

17
F-14A BuNo 159428 of VF-211, USS *John C Stennis* (CVN-74), Northern Arabian Sea, March 2002

18
F-14A BuNo 161612 of VF-211, USS *John C Stennis* (CVN-74), Northern Arabian Sea, April 2002

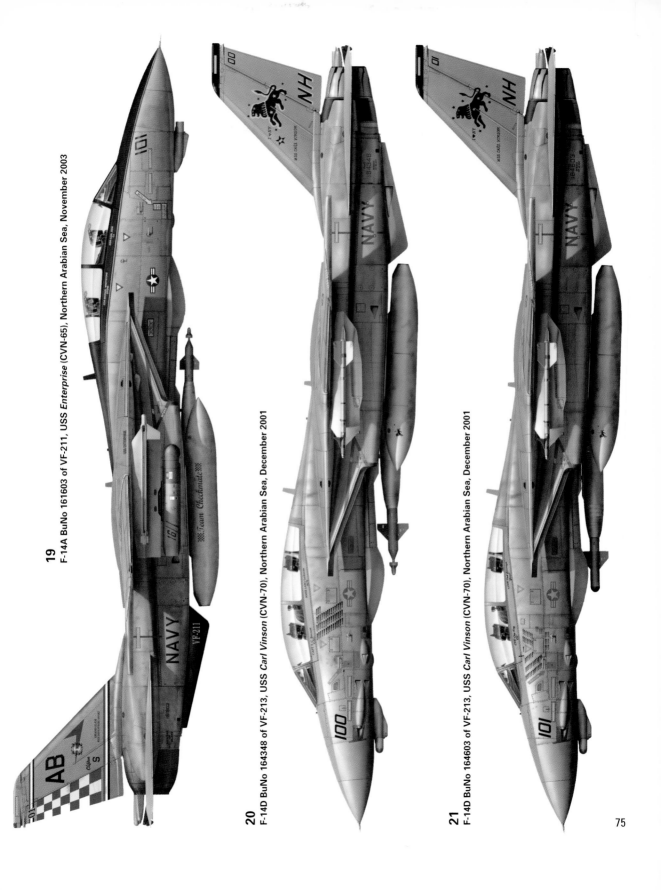

19
F-14A BuNo 161603 of VF-211, USS *Enterprise* (CVN-65), Northern Arabian Sea, November 2003

20
F-14D BuNo 164348 of VF-213, USS *Carl Vinson* (CVN-70), Northern Arabian Sea, December 2001

21
F-14D BuNo 164603 of VF-213, USS *Carl Vinson* (CVN-70), Northern Arabian Sea, December 2001

1

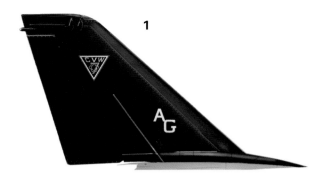

5

3

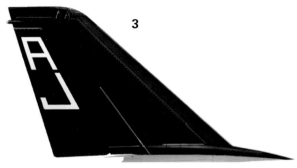

11

10

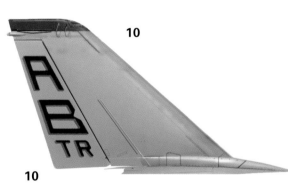

12

10

14

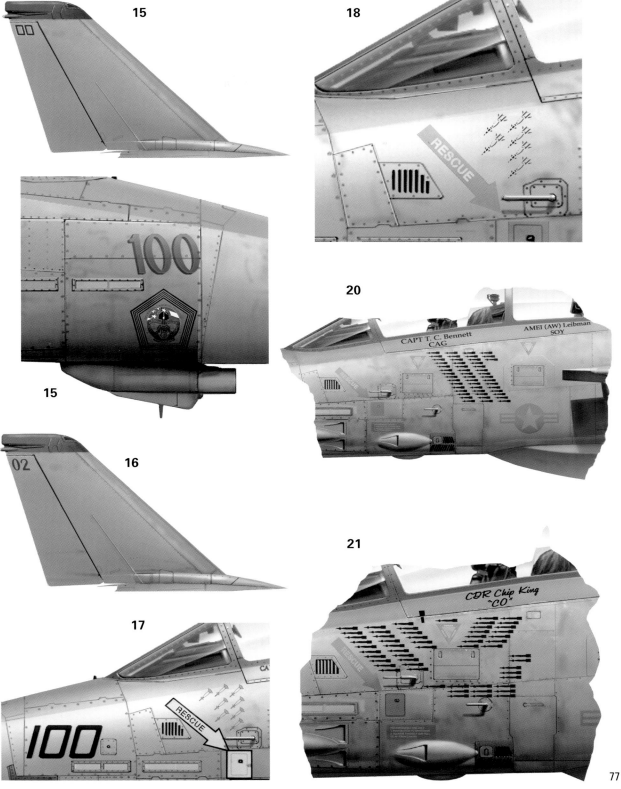

15

18

15

16

20

CAPT T. C. Bennett
CAG

AMEI (AW) Leibman
SOY

17

RESCUE

100

21

CDR Chip King
"CO"

RESCUE

OPERATION ANACONDA

By February 2002, CENTCOM commanders believed that most al-Qaeda fighters still in-country were holed up in the mountainous Shah-i-Kot region south of Gardez, in eastern Afghanistan's Paktia province. In what would eventually become the first major land battle of OEF involving a large number of American troops, the US Army's Task Force Mountain, consisting of 2000 soldiers from the 10th Mountain Division and 101st Airborne Division, together with Afghan forces, engaged up to 1000+ hardcore al-Qaeda fighters entrenched in ridgelines and caves throughout the Shah-i-Kot Valley.

Dubbed Operation *Anaconda*, the objectives of this campaign were supposed to have been achieved within 72 hours of it commencing, according to senior TF Mountain planners. In actuality, combat on the ground raged for two weeks, costing the lives of eight SOF team members and countless Afghan soldiers. A further 80 US troops were wounded.

The Army had seriously underestimated the size of the force opposing them. Spoiling for action, TF Mountain's opponents were battle-hardened Arab and Chechen fighters equipped with crew-served heavy machine guns, sniper rifles and mortars that were located in camouflaged positions in the mountains surrounding the Shah-i-Kot Valley. These men had plenty of provisions, as well as a robust communications system.

Although Coalition forces eventually prevailed in *Anaconda*, the battle was only won thanks to an overwhelming, and sustained, aerial bombardment. Ironically, no TACAIR assets were originally briefed into the *Anaconda* battle plan by TF Mountain, the Army instead choosing to rely on Apache helicopters. Having not been dialled into the operation, and therefore unaware of its scale, CTF-50 had allowed CVN-71 to have its first port call in 159 days on 28 February when the vessel briefly visited Bahrain. Key staff from CVW-9 were also in town, as Fifth Fleet was conducting a tactics review conference with TACAIR COs and operations officers from both air wings. Attending this event was VF-211's 'OPSO', Lt Cdr Nick Dienna;

'We should have realised that something was up when we were tasked with flying a series of TARPS missions over the Shah-i-Kot area in late February. Our frustration grew rapidly during the first two days of the campaign when we saw just how poorly the TACAIR aspects of the offensive had been planned. With

Home to battle-hardened enemy fighters, one of the many ridgelines bordering the Shah-i-Kot Valley is pounded by Tomcats and Hornets from CVW-9 during the opening stages of Operation *Anaconda* in March 2002. VF-211's Lt Cdr Nick Dienna recalled an early mission to this area. 'We were heading up to the Shah-i-Kot Valley when we were told by our E-2s that "Bossman" had new tasking for us along the nearby Afghan-Pakistan border. We were to destroy two vehicles containing al-Qaeda fighters that had been spotted trying to flee the country. By the time we arrived on-scene, it appeared as if World War 3 had broken out below us, with UAVs criss-crossing the target area and French Mirage 2000s conducting bombing runs – both vehicles had already been hit by then. We were cleared in to drop two LGBs apiece, which we did without any great fuss, and then headed back to the Shah-i-Kot and delivered our remaining ordnance. This mission was typical of most of our sorties during the *Anaconda* period. We would launch from the ship with briefed target areas to work in, but there was always a chance that we would be diverted elsewhere by "Bossman" to hit a TST' (*US Army*)

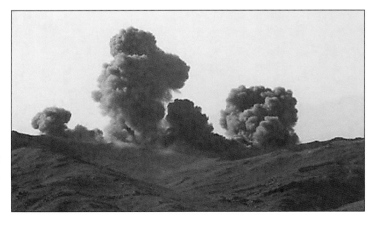

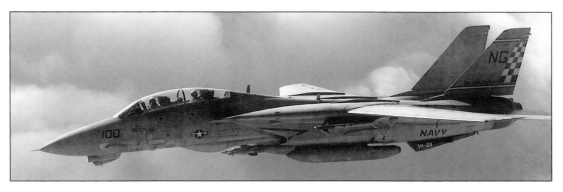

VF-211's 'Nickel 100' (BuNo 159428) cruises over cloud cover during *Anaconda*. Poor weather blighted CVW-9's OEF cruise, and it reduced the amount of ordnance that the 'Fighting Checkmates' dropped during the large-scale offensive in the Shah-i-Kot Valley because the unit's Tomcats were not JDAM-capable. This particular aircraft expended eight LGBs during VF-211's OEF cruise. Delivered to the Navy in October 1974 and intially flown by VF-124, BuNo 159428 joined VF-101 in December of the following year. It duly saw fleet service with VF-14 and VF-33, before spending time with Reserve-manned VF-201 and VF-202. Returning to VF-101 in the mid-1990s, the aircraft was transferred to VF-211 in 1998 and marked up as the unit's CAG jet. Having exhausted its airframe hours by early 2003, BuNo 159428 was scrapped in January 2004 (*Lt(jg) Mitch McAllister*)

A SEAL team use a grenade to mark a cave entrance for bombing in the Paktia province (*US Navy*)

most of the air wing leadership in town on the eve of *Anaconda*, we felt that CVW-9 could have at the very least rendered some assistance in the development of a plan for airspace control for prepping the battlefield. This would have given us insight into the aims of the campaign, and how the commanders on the ground wanted the battlefield to be shaped so as to achieve their goals expeditiously and with minimum casualties.'

VF-211's Lt Dan Buchar expressed the feelings of most aircrew aboard CVN-74 when he told the Author, 'The planning of *Anaconda* certainly left something to be desired in respect to naval aviation's contribution to the operation, as we were enjoying a rare beer day when it all kicked off!'

With USS *John F Kennedy* (CV-67) due in-theatre in early March as relief for CVN-71, CVN-74 had chosen 2 March to make the transition from night to day operations by declaring a no-fly day. CENTCOM had raised no objections when informed of this brief operational stand-down.

Anaconda had originally been due to start on 28 February, but it was delayed until 2 March due to poor weather. Just hours before troops moved into the Shah-i-Kot Valley, Lt Cdr Dienna and other senior officers in CVW-9 were briefed that the biggest OEF campaign since the air wing's arrival in-theatre was about to commence. 'My first questions as "OPSO" were "Where are the airspace control measures, where are we going and who are we supporting?" I received few answers from the CAOC', recalled Lt Cdr Dienna. 'The first two days of *Anaconda* reflected the fact that there had been little coordination between the 10th Mountain Division, which was running the offensive on the ground, and TACAIR assets in-theatre, which were in essence charged with supplying the aerial artillery for the troops.

'I experienced the lack of big picture airspace and tactical control during the early phase of the offensive at first hand when my section made ten runs through the Shah-i-Kot Valley trying to release our weapons. Each time we had Apaches come through beneath us working the valley, thus preventing us from getting our ordnance off.

'There were numerous SOF teams working throughout the Shah-i-Kot, and our primary

concern when we started flying *Anaconda* missions was our lack of knowledge as to their exact location. We would check in on a frequency with one JTAC and start working targets for him, without understanding what the overall battlespace looked like. It took CVW-9 a good 48 hours to get a handle on what was going on on the ground in the Shah-i-Kot.'

VF-102's FINAL MISSIONS

While CVW-9 was left kicking its heels for the first day of *Anaconda*, CVW-1, fresh from its port call, responded to anxious requests for help as TF Mountain troops came under withering machine gun and mortar fire when airlifted into the valley by Army CH-47s. Eight Apaches had been tasked with covering the insertion, but three were scrubbed pre-mission due to technical problems. The remaining five were immediately targeted by al-Qaeda fighters once in the valley, with every one of them being hit either by machine gun rounds or shrapnel from rocket-propelled grenades. Limping back to base, they were all declared unserviceable.

With air controllers on the ground bombarding the TF Mountain command cell in Bagram with anxious pleas for air support, the CAOC did its best to get jets into the area as quickly as possible. The call went out to CVW-1, and VF-102 was amongst the units to respond, launching four jets on what would prove to be the 'Diamondbacks'' last OEF mission. The RIO in the lead aircraft noted the details in his cruise diary;

'Somehow I conned the "OPSO" into including me in the unit's final OEF mission when we got the call to support Operation *Anaconda* – after

Between 17 September 2001 and 24 February 2002, CVN-71 and CVW-1 set a new Navy record for 159 continuous days at sea – the old record of 153 days had stood for 22 years. Large numbers personified the air wing's OEF cruise, with its aircraft flying 11,459 sorties, totalling 31,991 flight hours. Of those, 4078 sorties were in direct support of OEF. CVW-1 dropped 940 tons of conventional, laser-guided and GPS-guided munitions over five months, and achieved an outstanding 99 percent sortie-completion rate (*US Navy*)

VF-102's ten F-14Bs flew more than 5000 hours during the unit's OEF cruise – more than any other TACAIR unit in CVW-1. With the Tomcat averaging 60 to 70 maintenance hours per flying hour, the effort put in by the unit's support personnel (seen here in green, dark brown, red and white shirts) was nothing short of Herculean (*VF-102*)

months of no action, we were all certain that we would be getting bombs off on this flight. I convinced him because I had seven carryover missions from OSW, and this flight would be my 43rd for OEF, thus giving me 50 in total. This would earn me five strike/flight air medals post-cruise.

'I briefed the flight and we manned up five jets. This was just as well, as our planned wingman went down. The fourth Tomcat in our division had a bad LTS pod, but we took him in any case.

'The USAF had dropped plenty of JDAM in the area last night, but these had clearly been ineffective as we had received reports that several AH-64s had suffered battle damage earlier today. The flow into the area was orderly, and we were passed to a Ground FAC frequency, then switched to another with the call-sign "White Lightning". We were given coordinates for enemy bunkers, but got bogged down with a bad talk-on.

'Cloud covered the target area half of the time, but we had the FAC mark it with a M203 grenade launcher. Although his first round dudded, the second hit home, and I pulled the correction from him of "800 NW". Just as we were getting ready to throw some bombs down to get the ball rolling, "Dragon" (the Direct Air Support Center in Bagram) called the FAC and told him that his sensors in the area were picking up friendlies near the bunkers – not a good feeling at all. Here we were on the last day of our war, and they had tried to get us to kill some good guys.

'"White Lightning" then went off the air for a while, as he tried to unscrew his programme, so we talked to another Ground FAC. He passed us coordinates of a cave he wanted us to attack, but he couldn't see it. He had people observing it though, so we could get corrections, but they were delayed. Eventually, using our LTS pod, we found something ourselves that was close to his cave, and we and our wingman attacked it with a single LGB apiece. The FAC called the correction of 100 metres east. We then did another attack, putting the bombs 100 metres east as directed, and the next correction from the FAC was 300 metres east!

'We were getting low on fuel, so we handed the tasking off to the second section of Tomcats just as the FAC passed us a third target set – yet another one that he couldn't see, and with friendlies within 300 metres of the aim point. We declined and went off and stole some gas (about 4000 lbs each) from an off-going tanker, before all joining up at our last tanker. The Ground FACs were asking for guys to strafe as we were leaving, but the French E-2C took over from "Bossman" and had no clue. The good thing was another division of strikers was on station to give the guys support. We headed back to CVN-71 for the diamond break.'

The following day CVN-71 left the Northern Arabian Sea and set course for home. By then VF-102 had dropped 420,000 lbs of ordnance and buddy-lased an additional 50,000 lbs from other platforms. The unit had tallied 5000+ hours of flying time – more than any other TACAIR unit in CVW-1 – with 1184 hours in November alone, and a staggering 61.8 hours on 8 December in the lead up to the Tora Bora campaign.

'FIGHTING CHECKMATES' IN ACTION

On 3 March VF-211 at last got the chance to show its mettle in OEF, the unit's aviators having spent almost three months kicking their heels flying uneventful XCAS patrols over Afghanistan. Having missed the first day of *Anaconda*, the 'Fighting Checkmates' soon made up for lost time.

As had been the case earlier in OEF, FAC(A)s like Lt Cdr Nick Dienna, played a particularly important role in this chaotic offensive;

'In *Anaconda*, we had a much larger force than had previously been seen in Afghanistan operating in a much smaller area. A standard kill box controlled by one FAC at the start of OEF was 30 x 30 nautical miles, but in *Anaconda* that area had shrunk to 8 x 8 nautical miles, run by 30+ Coalition SOF, US SOF and TF Mountain controllers! With a larger friendly footprint on the ground, you now needed the more traditional controls that we strictly observed when conducting CAS training during work-ups. These did not exist in the early stages of *Anaconda*.

'Realising that there was no real airspace control plan for the offensive, our FAC(A) crews took it upon themselves to organise TACAIR support in their assigned target areas. They would check in on the primary control frequency given to them by "Bossman" and then try and get all other TACAIR assets in the immediate area to tune into this frequency too. Having determined who was talking to which FAC, and where they were located, they then went about deconflicting the strikers either laterally or vertically. This worked well, as the number of jets from CVW-9 in the Shah-i-Kot at any one time was manageable – typically two divisions.

'The first division would check in, with the second 45 minutes behind it. These would then alternate between the target area and the tanker so that there was always a two- or four-ship formation over the target the entire time. The divisions were typically mixed, with a single section of Tomcats being paired up with a similar number of Hornets. The latter were usually armed with JDAM and LMAVs, while the F-14s carried LGBs and iron bombs – a spread of weapons that CVW-9 found covered most targeting requirements. We would split up into sections once over the Shah-i-Kot due to the jets' differing tanking cycles. There were also some USAF F-15Es in the mix, but they tended to do their own thing.'

VF-211's most memorable day of fighting in OEF occurred on 4 March after a SOF team was ambushed soon after dawn as they attempted to insert themselves on the ridgeline of Takur Ghar. They were heading for Objective Ginger, which had a commanding view of the entire Shah-i-Kot Valley, but al-Qaeda forces in hardened, camouflaged, bunkers shot up their MH-47E just as it landed and forced the helicopter to hastily leave – crucially without Navy SEAL PO Neil Roberts.

When word reached Bagram that there was a soldier missing behind enemy lines, an Army Ranger quick reaction unit scrambled in two more

VF-211's CAG jet tops off its tanks with fuel passed by an RAF Tristar K 1 tanker from Omani-based No 216 Sqn in March 2002. All F-14 crews interviewed by the Author for this book were unanimous in their praise of the British tanker force in OEF. 'Tristars and VC10Ks were by far the best big wing tankers to get fuel from', VF-211 nugget pilot Lt(jg) Mitch McAllister remembered. 'They would happily descend and ease back on the throttles so as to accommodate us in military power. I always asked the USAF big wing tankers if they would slow down, and usually they answered in the negative – especially if we had hit them when they were still fully fuelled up with 100,000 lbs of gas onboard to give away.

'Being in an F-14A fitted with high bypass TF30 turbofan engines, refuelling at high altitude when fully bombed up could often be difficult due to the high airspeeds at which the tankers had to fly. We just did not have the throttle response with the TF30 to be up at 25,000 ft+ when loaded with four bombs. Routinely, once we got in the basket with our probe, we would slide our left throttle up into Zone Two or Three afterburner and just modulate the right throttle so as to stay in the basket – you just hoped that you were taking in more gas than you were burning. When the tanker went into a turn at the end of its track, the Tomcat would lose what little wing lift it had at this altitude and drop out of the basket. You would then have to wait until the tanker rolled out of its turn before jumping back into the basket again. Engine flame-outs and stalls on the tanker were commonplace for F-14A units in OEF' (*Lt(jg) M McAllister*)

MH-47Es. When the first of these touched down 50 metres from the top of Takur Ghar, the enemy again targeted the helicopter and shot it down through a combination of rocket-propelled grenade and machine gun fire. Four crewmen died and others were wounded, and survivors set up defensive positions just 150 metres from one of the snow-covered al-Qaeda bunkers. They were eventually rescued at 2000 hrs, having relied exclusively on CAS support to keep the enemy at bay. Their combat controller, USAF Capt Gabe Brown (call-sign 'Slick 01'), later told his superiors that he had handled 30 CAS sorties that day. Flying one of the jets near Takur Ghar was VF-211 pilot Lt Dan Buchar;

'Shortly after dawn, I launched as part of a division of four F-14s sent into Afghanistan in support of *Anaconda*, having been briefed to head to the Shah-i-Kot Valley to help troops in contact as they continued to battle with enemy forces. As we headed north, the SOF MH-47E was shot down near Objective Ginger. Shortly after that, our division lead, Lt Larry Sidbury, got a call from "Bossman" telling him that our bombs were needed straight away. We had to refuel first, however, so each jet quickly topped off its tanks and then headed independently to the target area.

'Lt Sidbury and his RIO, Lt Cdr Tim Fitzpatrick, who were both FAC(A)-qualified, reached Takur Ghar first and made contact with "Slick 01". The latter was pinned down near the wreckage of the MH-47 along with the survivors of the Army Ranger quick reaction unit. Lt Sidbury and his wingman, Lt Bryan Roberts, worked directly with "Slick 01", and they dropped ordnance within 500 metres of the friendlies.

'Ordered to return to the ship by the AWACS after dropping all of his bombs, Lt Sidbury told everybody – including a rear admiral and a USAF general – "No" because the guys in the ground were still taking fire. He got the point where he turned his radios off, thus blocking out the distraction of the "return to base" calls. Eventually relieved on station, Lt Sidbury somehow made it to the tanker before running out of fuel and recovered aboard CVN-74.

'His CO was still flying at the time, but his XO started grilling him about why he had ignored the calls to return. At this point CAG stormed into the ready room and started to tear strips of Lt Sidbury for disobeying a direct order. A few minutes later the admiral also walked in, and everybody immediately stood to attention. His first words to Lt Sidbury were, "That's the best thing I ever saw. Don't you ever do anything different"!

'Nickel 100' formates at high altitude with a JDAM-armed B-52H from the 23rd Bombardment Squadron (BS)/5th Bombardment Wing (BW), forward-deployed to Diego Garcia from Minot AFB, North Dakota. Ten B-52s were based on the atoll in the Indian Ocean from the very start of OEF, aircraft from the 2nd (Barksdale AFB, Louisiana) and 5th BWs taking it in turns to undertake temporary tours of duty with the 28th Air Expeditionary Wing (AEW). The latter also controlled B-1Bs and KC-10As operating from the same base. Typically, the 28th AEW would generate five B-52 OEF sorties a day (*Lt(jg) Mitch McAllister*)

The 'Whaleback' was the dominant feature within the Shah-i-Kot Valley, and it was also the scene of some of the fiercest fighting in *Anaconda* (*USAF*)

"Whaleback"

'While Lt Sidbury and his wingman had been controlling the airspace over Takur Ghar, my RIO, Lt Cdr Ed Galvin, and I, along with Lt Mark Bruington and his RIO, Lt Shaun Swartz, had been sent to attack mortar positions firing on our troops in the south-eastern corner of the Shah-i-Kot Valley. We got to work with an EP-3E rather than a JTAC during this mission, with targeting information being fed to us by the aircraft as we circled over the valley. The EP-3E had a SOF guy in the back picking out the mortar positions with the Orion's sensors. The descriptions that he gave us as to the location of the mortars were eye-watering in detail! He would say "do you see the mud hut with the courtyard?" as he tried to talk us onto a building whilst we were circling at 20,000 ft! The mortars were actually within mud huts on the edge of the town of Shah-i-Kot itself.

'After we failed to locate the target, the EP-3E had a B-1 that was on station throw a JDAM down to act as a mark for us. My RIO quickly spotted the impact point on the FLIR, and the SOF guy also talked his eyes onto it, and we hit the mortar pit and two vehicles with a pair of LGBs. Their destruction was confirmed by the EP-3E, and we then targeted another position with our remaining GBU-12s. All four jets in our division returned to CVN-74 without their bombs.

'There was also a Predator UAV on station near the EP-3E, as well as the B-1, and some F-15Es checked in just as we left. It was an all-out effort to provide TACAIR coverage for the guys pinned down on Takur Ghar, as well as our troops coming under fire in the valley below.

'Things had gotten a little frantic for a while there when we were struggling to locate the mortar position. We actually had the B-1 split our section at one point as Lt Bruington was working the target area and I was providing high cover for him – the bomber flew between us. It was after this that we decided that we needed to get altitude separations between aircraft types sorted out before we bombed anything! We decided to stick to individual CAP points that were widely spaced, and only came into the valley when instructed to by the EP-3E. We never actually saw the Orion during this mission, the aircraft being higher than us, and some distance away from the valley. We did, however, spot the UAV, which was down at 10,000 ft, while we stuck to a hard deck height of 20,000 ft.'

IRON BOMBS

As Lt Cdr Dienna mentioned earlier in this chapter, VF-211 started carrying a mixed load of two LGBs and two general purpose iron bombs soon after the start of *Anaconda*. As with other F-14 units that had used GP ordnance in OEF, the 'Fighting Checkmates' predominantly uploaded 500-lb Mk 82 or 1000-lb Mk 83 TDD-fused bombs to ensure maximum area coverage against troops in the open or in shallow trenches.

'VF-211 had not dropped any GP bombs up until then in the deployment', Lt Cdr Dienna told the Author. 'Iron bombs were often used for reconnaissance-by-fire purposes, marking out targets for LGBs. We always tried to get the GP bombs off as soon as we checked in, rolling in at a 45-degree-angle once cleared to drop in the Shah-i-Kot Valley. We would then wait for any on-call tasking for our LGBs, which were typically aimed at high value targets, or targets where there were collateral damage issues. A number of them were also dropped in fire-for-effect situations, rather than against specific targets'.

One of the first naval aviators from VF-211 to drop a GP bomb in anger also happened to be VF-211's newest pilot. 'I joined the "Fighting Checkmates" with just 30 hours in the A-model Tomcat in my logbook, having been trained to fly the F-14B for much of my time in VF-101', recalled Lt(jg) Kevin Robb. 'I was scheduled to join a B-squadron, but they needed a priority F-14A student graduate to join VF-211. I got my deck qualification in the jet with VF-101 off the Norfolk coast on a Monday and was then sent by civil airliner to Bahrain four days later. I started flying combat missions within 24 hours of my arrival on CVN-74, and less than a week after getting deck qualified in the F-14A!

'My bomb-dropping mission came about a week into *Anaconda*. As with previous sorties I had flown in OEF, we launched in the late afternoon as a section of Tomcats designated as an XCAS asset, without a pre-planned target. As soon as the skipper checked in with "Bossman" at our allocated loiter time, he was told that there was urgent tasking for us. We were instructed to call a JTAC, who in turn gave us coordinates for a road north of the Shah-i-Kot Valley that he had had under surveillance.

'Enemy forces were retreating back into the mountains in cars and trucks, and the JTAC wanted the road severed and some vehicles travelling on it hit so as to block it off as an escape route for al-Qaeda/Taleban fighters. Time was of the essence here, and we were given immediate approval to drop by "Bossman" once overhead the target area. My skipper asked the JTAC where and when he wanted the bombs, and as his wingman, it was my job to listen carefully to the instructions that the CO was given, for I would attack immediately after him.

'I remained in a high cover position – with a 30-degree angle of bank – for the skipper as he rolled in and dropped his ordnance, and I then worked off his hits. Indeed, the JTAC told me to put both of my bombs directly on top of my CO's, so that's what I did. We came in on the road at an angle of 50 degrees, some 45 degrees off the target itself, which was pretty exciting to say the least – VF-101 hadn't really prepared me for dive-bombing targets with unguided ordnance from such a high altitude and at such a steep angle. We had to roll in from around 30,000 ft simply because the terrain in the area was so high. The road, which was carved into the side of a mountain, was at about 6000 ft MSL.

'My compatriots had been almost exclusively dropping GBU-12s up until this mission simply because of the nature of the CAS sorties they were performing, and the awesome targeting capabilities of the LTS. Therefore, I was convinced that if I got to drop any ordnance in OEF, it would be an LGB. When the JTAC asked for Mk 82s, I quickly studied my kneeboard Z-diagram and figured out the best attack profile to employ. I also confirmed my proposed course of action with my RIO, who was one of the more experienced back-seaters in the unit.

'With an LGB delivery, the RIO would have done most of the work, designating the target with the LTS pod. However, as I had already realised, he told me that the success of this attack was entirely in my hands. He played his part by talking my eyes onto my CO's bomb hits, and that helped me get lined up with the target. My RIO expended chaff and flares as we dived on the target, and also when we pulled out.

'Fortunately, the weather was glorious, as the skipper kept reminding me. He could not believe that I was going to get to drop ordnance for the

first time in an angle-dive attack in gin clear conditions. This was the first time that Cdr Kovacich had dropped Mk 82s in anger as well.

'We expended both of our Mk 82s in pairs, as the JTAC wanted them as quickly as possible. He then responded with "Good Effects" after both runs, and we left the area. By the time I got back to the boat, we had been airborne for five-and-a-half hours, making this my longest OEF mission. This was the only time I dropped bombs on cruise.

'We carried two GBU-12s and two Mk 82s on most *Anaconda* missions, as we could trap back aboard with this configuration should the bombs have not been needed. For night missions, we would switch to four GBU-12s, as it was difficult to accurately aim dumb bombs in the dark. We also carried GBU-16s early on in the cruise, and these were again uploaded during *Anaconda*, when crews knew that they would be definitely dropping ordnance.

'We were flying old F-14s in 2002, and our maintenance folks did a great job keeping them airworthy. We lost a jet on 8 March when its hook separated on landing, but the crew punched out okay. During the course of that particular day, we had managed to sortie eight of our ten jets!'

This was the second Tomcat lost in less than a week, as on 2 March VF-143's 'Dog 101' had suffered a nose gear strut failure while launching from CV-67 off Crete. Although the RIO managed to eject safely, the pilot of the F-14B, Lt Cdr Chris Blaschum, was killed. Following the crash, 'all Tomcats were grounded so that their nose gear could be checked for the type of fatigue cracks that had caused the undercarriage to fail during its catapult shot', recalled VF-143's Lt(jg) Joseph Greentree.

'Airframers in the maintenance departments of both Tomcat units in CVW-7 worked round the clock removing nose gear legs and inspecting them. They managed to turn all the aircraft around in just 72 hours. Soon after we arrived in-theatre, VF-211 then lost a jet when its tailhook separated, and again we were grounded for three days while our jets were inspected and passed fit to fly.

'Theses failures were rather disconcerting, because I remember one of my instructors in VF-101 telling me that the two things that would never break on this aircraft were the nose gear and the tailhook! Both failures were put down to undetectable corrosion caused by the sheer age of the jets involved.'

The VF-143 crash was the latest in a list of unfortunate events that had blighted CV-67 and CVW-7 in

Four storeless VF-211 jets join up in close formation for their run in and break over CVN-74 in late March 2002. Both 'Nickel 101' (BuNo 161603) and '102' (BuNo 162612) boast bomb tallies beneath their cockpits. The canopy rails of each VF-211 jet bore the names of New York Police and Fire Department personnel killed on 11 September 2001 (*Lt(jg) Mitch McAllister*)

'Nickel 102' leads 'Nickel 101' into CVN-74's overhead prior to joining the landing pattern. This photograph was taken shortly after *Anaconda* had reached its climax. The completion of the offensive effectively brought to an end all bomb dropping in Afghanistan, which is why both jets are still carrying four GBU-12s. Lighter than the F-14B/D, the A-model jet could land back aboard in quad bomber configuration (*Lt(jg) M McAllister*)

the lead up to their OEF deployment. In an unprecedented move, the ship's captain had been relieved of his command when 'JFK' failed its Board of Inspection Survey in December 2001 – a decision which delayed the ship's departure on cruise. The *Kennedy* battle group also initially failed its Joint Task Force Exercise, which CVW-7 had had to undertake 'from the beach' because CV-67 was still in Mayport being prepared for deployment. The vessel finally sailed on 16 February 2002.

CVW-7 conducted a theatre turnover with CVW-1 as 'TR' and 'JFK' passed each other in the Red Sea, and VF-11 and VF-143 made their OEF debuts over Afghanistan on 11 March. CVW-7 had been given the job of night carrier, and it launched its first wave of 11 aircraft in the early hours of the morning on the 11th. Heading for the Shah-i-Kot Valley, the jets were 'set up for heavy FAC(A) and CAS targets' according to VF-11 CO, Cdr John Aquilino. One of these aircraft was also making history for the Tomcat, as it was equipped with a single 2000-lb GBU-31 JDAM.

GPS-guided J-weapons had been introduced to the fleet by the F/A-18C during Operation *Allied Force* in the spring of 1999. By early 2001, NAVAIR had engineered a software upgrade for the F-14B which would allow the jet to employ JDAM. VF-102 was too far progressed in its work-up cycle to have the software fitted into its jets, so CVW-7's two Tomcat units were the first ones to receive the upgrade.

'Nickel 104' (BuNo 158618) accelerates down CVN-74's waist cat four in Zone Five afterburner during an early *Anaconda* mission. This aircraft was lost on 8 March 2002 when its tailhook separated on landing at the completion of an OEF mission. Both crewmen successfully ejected. Delivered to the Navy in October 1972, and having spent many years in the Tomcat test programme with VX-4, the jet was refurbished in the early 1980s and issued to VF-201. It finally reached the fleet in 1998, some 26 years after entering service with the Navy, when it joined VF-211 (*US Navy*)

VF-11's 'Ripper 210' jousts with a KC-135 over Afghanistan during *Anaconda*. Attached to its forward port belly pallet is a GBU-31 JDAM, and this weapon was employed in anger by a Tomcat (from VF-11) for the very first first time on 11 March 2002 (*Lt Brian Vanyo*)

The VF-11 JDAM jet sortied on 11 March was flown by Lt Cdrs Scott Knapp and Chris Chope, who Cdr Aquilino described as 'the most qualified naval aviators in the unit when it came to J-weapon employment, having done most of VF-11's integration work with the GBU-31'. Once on station over the Shah-i-Kot Valley, the section of 'Ripper' jets was told by a JTAC to bomb a mortar pit near the 'Whale-back'. 'We set up a trail attack profile whereby our wingman would drop his GBU-12 first and we would drop the JDAM moments later through the smoke created by his weapon', recalled Lt Cdr Chope.

'Seen through our LTS pod, his weapon skipped off a rock and exploded alongside the target. When it came time for us to pickle our GBU-31, however, the weapon hung, refusing to leave the jet. Lt Cdr Knapp and I did everything by the book, but it refused to drop. After a silent flight back to the ship, we landed and the armourers removed the GBU-31 from the jet and tested it, whereupon the bomb was found to be faulty. The guidance unit in the tail kit, which has its own GPS receiver and navigation system, was not talking to the jet's weapons computer.'

The following night CVW-7 conducted more OEF sorties, with Cdr Aquilino and his RIO, Lt Cdr Kevin Protzman, leading a VF-11 section;

'We were cleared to hit a cave complex on the "Whaleback", having already been given a rough target set aboard the ship. Once on station, we received support from an E-8 JSTARS that was circling overhead the Shah-i-Kot, as well as aim point GPS coordinates for our JDAM from "Bossman". My RIO punched the numbers into his mission computer and then reread them back to the AWACS controller to confirm that he had typed them in correctly. Only then were we given approval to release the bomb. We made our run in on the target from high altitude and recorded good BHA video of the weapon hitting the cave entrance.

'We later heard from troops in the area that they had been impressed by the strikes flown that night, with all the targets that they had identified being hit. The cave complex burned for about 12 hours.

'Our jet was carrying a solitary GBU-31, as at that time we only had clearance to drop the 2000-lb weapon – we were yet to receive permission to pair the JDAM with an LGB or a dumb bomb. With targets being at a premium, we decided that there was no point in taking two JDAM, as we would have had to jettison one in the water in order to get down to our minimum landing weight if we failed to find anyone who needed our bombs. We didn't have too many GBU-31s in the armoury at that time, so jettisoning ordnance was not an option.'

By the time CV-67 arrived in-theatre, the land component running *Anaconda* had streamlined its airpower coordination plan. Keen to get more bombs on target, TF Mountain made sure that it supplied the CAOC with a list of pre-planned target coordinates for strike aircraft to use in case of bad weather or shortening vul times. With an E-8 JSTARS also on station scouring the valley, TST coordinates were now reaching TACAIR crews much quicker too.

The offensive to take Objective Ginger on 9 March was the culmination of *Anaconda*, and it saw 667 weapons dropped in just 48 hours. By 16 March all the objectives that TF Mountain had hoped to complete during *Anaconda* had at last been achieved, with the Shah-i-Kot Valley cleared of enemy forces.

TOMCAT FINALE

ollowing the successful conclusion of Operation *Anaconda*, and the apparent disintegration of the Taleban as a credible fighting force in Afghanistan, CENTCOM scaled back its operations in OEF. As part of this drawdown, CTF-50 was reduced in strength to a single carrier battle group from 18 April 2002, when CVN-74 and CVW-9 left the Northern Arabian Sea and headed home. VF-211 had expended close to 100,000 lbs of ordnance in OEF, with almost all of this being dropped during *Anaconda* – CVW-9 expended 350,000 lbs in total. The unit's F-14As had flown 1250 missions (the air wing totalled 3242) and logged 4200 hours in combat over Afghanistan (CVW-9 tallied 13,500 combat hours), with VF-211's maintenance department coaxing a 99.7 percent sortie completion rate from its charges.

With the departure of CVN-74, CVW-7 now provided the primary TACAIR presence in-theatre. Afghanistan was very quiet throughout 2002, however, as VF-11's Lt Cdr Chris Chope explained to the Author;

'When things petered out after 16 March, it was tough for CVW-7 just to sit on the line for the next four months and see next to no action. I was FAC(A)-qualified, which meant that I spent a lot of time operating with troops in the field, as well as other TACAIR assets such as B-52s and B-1s. The air control parties on the ground were clearly working hard while we were in country, as you could hear these guys panting as they ran up and down mountains trying to stay in radio contact with us.

'Communicating with troops on the ground was tough in OEF due to the size of the mountains over which we were often flying. If you got on the wrong side of a peak from where the JTAC was situated, you would lose contact. Trying to visually acquire a team of six or seven guys in mountainous terrain was also a challenge, and I only saw them very occasionally through binoculars or with the LTS. Despite having no visual reference on their position, we usually had a good feel for where the SOF teams were, and we would help them out by scouting the area ahead of them in advance of their movement on the ground.

'In our capacity as a FAC(A) crew, my pilot and I would routinely operate with Marine Corps F/A-18Ds and USAF A-10s from Manas, in Kyrgystan, P-3C/EP-3Es from Masirah Island, off Oman, F-15Es and F-16s from Al Udeid, in Qatar, B-1Bs from Seeb, in Oman, and B-52Hs from Diego Garcia and Guam. Crews would check in once on station, and we would occasionally ask them to go and investigate a contact raised by a JTAC, after which they would hit the tanker and head home.'

With the need for LGBs and JDAM having gone, at least for now, high-speed show-of-force flybys soon became the order of the day. 'This was not a mission that we had been trained to fly pre-cruise, as it had never appeared in our work-up syllabus', recalled VF-11 CO Cdr John Aquilino. 'We had been told by VF-102 during our OEF turnover that flybys would soon feature regularly in our mission tasking. VF-211 emphasised this point too, explaining to us that although such flybys may

VF-11's Lt Cdr Chris Chope and his pilot take on mid-mission fuel from a KC-10 during an OEF patrol in May 2002. 'You would raise the tanker on the radio to find out where he was and then you would lock it up with your radar', Lt Cdr Chope once recalled. 'Having rendezvoused with the tanker, you would ask him to reel out the drogue, and once this was in position, you would extend your probe and plug in. If you were a little short on fuel, or you needed to be back on station ASAP, you could ask the pilot of the tanker to roll out onto a certain heading so as to drag you closer to your objective while you were still plugged in replenishing your tanks. Most crews were pretty good at accommodating such requests, although the USAF guys did not like to stray too far off their designated tanker tracks. Some crews were so obliging that they would even do the leg work with the AWACS in respect to letting the controller know that they were moving from one track to another' (*Lt Cdr Chris Chope*)

not have seemed to be too big a deal from the crew's perspective, they meant a lot to the soldiers on the ground. When crowds were gathering near troops on patrol, and their intention was unknown, the fact that there were US jets in the air overhead that could have a direct impact on the situation was greatly appreciated by Coalition forces.

'With months of experience in-country, our troops had supplied the CAOC with feedback via "Bossman" on how they could get the most value out of our flybys. We were told that it was crucial to find an area near to the disturbance where the jet's engines could clearly be heard – it didn't matter if the aircraft could not actually be seen by friendly troops. A successful flyby was one that dispersed a crowd or helped buy the soldiers time to get a better understanding of what the crowd was going to do.

'I was asked to perform just one show-of-force flyby, and this was during a marathon ten-hour daylight mission. Patrolling northern Afghanistan, we were assigned a CAP station and a frequency for a ground FAC. Having checked in with him, we then waited during our vul window to provide this guy with whatever he needed – weapons on target, a show-of-force or just a presence in the sky above him.

'After 20 minutes of silence, he got back on the radio and asked us to fly a show-of-force. He passed us the latitude and longitude for the flyby, what direction he wanted us to come in from, the height we were cleared down to and any known threats in the area. We set up our jets in a two-aeroplane defensive spread for mutual support and optimum threat coverage, and then each of us took it in turns to make a single high-speed, subsonic pass with the afterburners "cooking" so as to make lots of noise. We pumped out plenty of flares during the runs too just in case there were any MANPADS in the immediate area.'

Very occasionally, CVW-7 would be called on to back up all this noise with a little muscle, and VF-143 pilot Lt Bill Mallory was one of only a handful of naval aviators to drop ordnance post-*Anaconda*;

'I was the wingman in a section of "Dog" jets patrolling near Kabul during a seemingly routine night XCAS mission at the midway point in our OEF cruise. Our jet (my RIO was squadron XO, Cdr Christopher Murray) was armed with two GBU-16s, and the lead aircraft, flown by Lt Cdrs Jonathan Stevenson and Matt Leahey, carried a single GBU-31.

'The launch, rendezvous and transit through Pakistan into Afghanistan went as it had done a dozen times before, and it was becoming a real challenge not to

'Ripper 207' (BuNo 161437) loses altitude over the Northern Arabian Sea as the crew prepare to recover aboard CV-67 following a Unit-Level Training (ULT) flight. With OEF missions being a priority for TACAIR units, ULT hops rarely featured on the daily flight plan once the air wing was committed to CTF-50 operations. When time allowed, sorties to a weapons range in Oman were undertaken so as to keep crews current on bomb delivery methods. These flights became increasingly more important after March 2002, as so little ordnance was being dropped in Afghanistan. It was a 200-mile transit flight from the carrier to the range, where crews dropped a mix of blue 25-lb practice bombs and laser-guided training rounds (*Lt Brian Vanyo*)

VF-143's CAG jet (BuNo 163220) is seen here over Afghanistan carrying a mixed bomb load consisting of a GBU-31 JDAM and a GBU-12 LGB. Clearance to carry such a loadout only reached CVW-7 from NAVAIR mid-cruise (*Lt Bill Mallory*)

lose interest in these missions. Therefore, when the AWACS controller told us that he wanted us to head to a particular kill box, we were ecstatic. It was readily apparent from their radio comms that Lt Cdrs Stevenson and Leahey really wanted to drop their very first JDAM, but the controller didn't want any more than 1000 lbs of ordnance, so Cdr Murray and I were in luck, and we were passed the lead.

'Unfortunately, either incorrect coordinates or a well hidden target, coupled with the functionality of the new 40K LTS pods that were fitted to our jets, gave us a hell of a time when it came to finding the aim point for our weapon. This led to too much "FLIR fishing", which was disorienting for both my RIO and I. We were quickly running out of our allotted vul time (which was just 15 minutes), so when Lt Cdr Leahey thought he had acquired the target in question, we passed the lead back to him and Lt Cdr Stevenson and executed a "buddy bomb" attack. As far as the target goes, if it was a rock, then we got a direct hit. We accomplished all that was asked of us, covering the egress of a SOF unit. Unfortunately, we dropped more external fuel tanks than bombs on this cruise.'

CV-67 and CVW-7 ended their OEF tour of duty on 19 July 2002 when they were relieved by USS *George Washington* (CVN-73) and CVW-17. While on station in the Northern Arabian Sea, CVW-7 had completed 2599 combat missions and expended 64,000 lbs of ordnance.

F-14B-equipped VF-103 was CVW-17's sole Tomcat unit, and it commenced flying XCAS, TARPS and FAC(A) missions over Afghanistan on 20 July. That very day, the unit came close to strafing a Taleban compound, as pilot Lt Cdr Lou Schager explained to the Author;

'Having just landed back aboard the ship from my first OEF mission, I was in CVIC listening to the radio chat from our relief section on station when I heard one of the pilots say that they had been called in to strafe a compound in support of troops in contact in northern Afghanistan. A short while later, however, the same individual came back up on the radio and reported that the cannon in the lead jet had jammed when the very first round got stuck in the breech. To make matters worse, the pilot in the second F-14 then had a HUD failure so he couldn't strafe either!

'Hornets from VFA-83 ended up doing some strafing, and a section of jets from VFA-81 then dropped two dumb bombs on the enemy position, leaving our guys to supply the light strike pilots with some good situational awareness about what was going on on the ground.

'The squadron felt great frustration at having not been able to strafe when the opportunity presented itself, and to make matters worse, this

'Ordies' from VF-103 load 20 mm SAFHEI rounds into the magazine of an F-14B on the deck of CVN-73. A gun jam on 20 July 2002 ruined VF-103's one and only chance to see combat in OEF (*US Navy*)

VF-103's CAG jet returns to CVN-73 with its two GBU-12s still very much in place in August 2002. Assigned to VF-102 in July 1988 upon its delivery to the Navy, this aircraft joined VF-101 eight years later, and was eventually assigned to VF-103 in early 2000. Marked up as the unit's CAG jet, it subsequently completed three combat tours (2000, 2002 and 2004) with the squadron. The Tomcat was retired to AMARC on 5 January 2005 (*Capt Dana Potts*)

was the only chance that VF-103 would get to employ ordnance during the OEF phase of its 2002 cruise. The unit had little choice but to chalk it up as a good lesson learned, and I know that our "ordies" and aviation technicians couldn't have felt any worse about the situation.'

CVN-73 headed west into the Northern Arabian Gulf (NAG) in early September, and CVW-17 immediately commenced OSW missions. This was the first time that carrier aircraft had flown into southern Iraq since CVW-8 had gone in-country on 9 September 2001. CVN-72 and CVW-14 then became the OEF carrier, with the air wing's VF-31 flying over Afghanistan between 11 September and 28 October 2002, prior to heading into the NAG. Like VF-103, VF-31 expended no ordnance.

VF-211 became the last Tomcat unit to fly OEF missions when it got the call to participate in Operation *Mountain Resolve* in early November 2003. A number of its naval aviators had previously seen combat during the unit's 2001-02 deployment, VF-211 having since switched air wings from CVW-9 to CVW-1. One of those was pilot Lt Dan Buchar;

'We were hastily pulled out of a port call to Dubai and rushed to the Northern Arabian Sea, where we were tasked with flying night missions. The CAOC wanted one FAC(A) crew per section over the beach, and that really hit a small number of our naval aviators hard – VF-211 only had four suitably qualified crews at the time. I pulled the 0200 hrs to 0800 hrs FAC(A) watch with my RIO, which was not a lot of fun – CVW-1 ran the FAC window at night and Bagram-based A-10s ran it during the day.

'I got to fly a couple of show-of-force passes during this period, where we were cleared down to 3000 ft – these were the standout missions for me during the 12 days that we supported *Mountain Resolve*. We flew some very long sorties lasting more than nine hours at a time, and I undertook three of these in a 72-hour period, all at night, as the CAOC wanted round-the-clock FAC(A) cover in-theatre. They set up E-2C and EA-6B dets at Bagram in support of *Mountain Resolve*, but had the TACAIR assets flying from the boat. The operation was well executed by CVW-1, but our troops failed to find any worthwhile targets for us to bomb.'

RIO Lt Mario Duarte also flew a number of OEF missions during *Mountain Resolve*, stating that the jet's 'LTS pod made the F-14 a critical tool for the CAOC during this operation, as it was the best infrared sensor in-theatre when it came to searching for vehicles or people moving at night. If something was detected, we would remain on station overhead and use different fields of view and polarities to work out who was moving on the roads below. The Coalition was keen to stop people travelling at will across the central border area with Pakistan'.

The last section of Tomcats to patrol over Afghanistan trapped back aboard *Enterprise* soon after dawn on 14 November 2003, thus bringing to an end the veteran Grumman fighter's considerable contribution to Operation *Enduring Freedom*.

VF-211 was the only Tomcat unit to make a return visit to Afghan skies, the 'Fighting Checkmates' participating in Operation *Mountain Resolve* in early November 2002. By then the squadron had transferred from CVW-9 to CVW-1, and was embarked in CVN-65. VF-211's commitment to the operation was to last just 12 days, with the Tomcat bidding OEF farewell for the last time on 14 November 2003 (*US Navy*)

APPENDICES

US NAVY F-14 TOMCAT UNITS INVOLVED IN OPERATION *ENDURING FREEDOM*

CVW-1 (USS *Theodore Roosevelt* (CVN-71))

VF-102 'DIAMONDBACKS' (F-14B)

161432/100	162692/105	163217/111	161608/115
163225/102	162910/106	162694/112	
161440/104	163407/110*	161422/114	

* sent to VF-143 on 7/3/02 as replacement for jet lost on 2/3/02

CVW-1 (USS *Enterprise* (CVN-65))

VF-211 'FIGHTING CHECKMATES' (F-14A)

161612/100	158632/103	158628/110	161297/115
161603/101	158635/104	161295/111*	
162610/102	161626/105	161275/114	

* declared written-off following mid-air collision over Red Sea with BuNo 158635 on 2 February 2004. Both jets landed safely aboard CVN-65

CVW-7 (USS *John F Kennedy* (CV-67))

VF-11 'RED RIPPERS' (F-14B)

161433/200	163408/203	162925/206	162919/211
162912/201	163218/204	161437/207	163409/212
161418/202	162927/205	162911/210	

VF-143 'PUKIN' DOGS' (F-14B)

163220/100	161438/102	162926/105	162701/111
162923/101*	161426/103	161434/106	161870/112
163407/101**	161873/104	161441/110	162924/114

* jet lost 2/3/02 in fatal crash off Crete

** replacement jet received from VF-102 on 7/3/02, this aircraft having previously been AB110

CVW-8 (USS *Enterprise* (CVN-65))

VF-14 'TOPHATTERS' (F-14A)

162698/200	162604/203	158624/206	161603/211
161279/201	161863/204	161292/207	161284/212
161607/202	158633/205	158632/210	

VF-41 'BLACK ACES' (F-14A)

161274/100	158612/103	161294/106	161168/113
162608/101	158630/104	161296/111	161275/114
161856/102	161615/105	161626/112	

CVW-9 (USS *John C Stennis* (CVN-74))

VF-211 'FIGHTING CHECKMATES' (F-14A)

159428/100	158632/103	161295/111	161297/115
161603/101	158618/104*	158637/112	
162612/102	158628/110	161622/114	

* jet lost 8/3/02 in non-fatal crash in Northern Arabian Sea

CVW-11 (USS *Carl Vinson* (CVN-70))

VF-213 'BLACK LIONS' (F-14D)

164348/100	163899/103	163893/106	161159/111
164603/101	159628/104	164344/107	164350/114*
163901/102	161163/105	164347/110	

* ex-VF-2 NE103, which was left behind in Kuwait in 8/01 due to bulkhead failure near tailhook during attempted recovery on CV-64 in the NAG. Damage was repaired by VF-213 maintenance team flown ashore in 9/01, and jet then flown to CVN-70. Aircraft flew a handful of combat missions, then handed back to VF-2 upon VF-213's return to NAS Oceana in 12/01

CVW-14 (USS *Abraham Lincoln* (CVN-72))

VF-31 'TOMCATTERS' (F-14D)

164601/100	164344/103	164343/106	163895/111
164600/101	163898/104	163413/107	
163904/102	159610/105	159618/110	

CVW-17 (USS *George Washington* (CVN-73))

VF-103 'JOLLY ROGERS' (F-14B)

162918/100	161435/103	161862/107	161855/112
162910/101	161442/104	163221/110	
161419/102	163229/105	162695/111	

COLOUR PLATES

1
F-14B BuNo 161433 of VF-11, USS *John F Kennedy* (CV-67), May 2002

Delivered new to VF-142 in November 1982, this aircraft subsequently became the seventh A-model jet upgraded to F-14A+ specification in the late 1980s. Returned to VF-142, the fighter remained with the unit until the 'Ghostriders'' were disestablished in April 1995. BuNo 161433 was then transferred to VF-103, and three years later it joined VF-11 as the unit's CAG jet. A veteran of two combat cruises with the 'Red Rippers', the Tomcat went to VF-101 following VF-11's OEF deployment and was scrapped at NAS Oceana on 10 March 2005 as part of the Stricken Aircraft Reclamation and Disposal Program (SARDIP).

2
F-14B BuNo 162912 of VF-11, USS *John F Kennedy* (CV-67), May 2002

Marked up with VF-11 anniversary titling on its twin fins, BuNo 162912 had joined this unit from VF-143 in 1997 when the 'Red Rippers' transitioned from D-model Tomcats to F-14Bs following their move from NAS Miramar to NAS Oceana. Originally delivered to the Navy in November 1988, the aircraft had served with VF-24, VF-101, VF-102, VF-142 and VF-143 prior to being issued to VF-11. Following three combat tours with the unit, BuNo 162912 was retired to the Grissom AFB Museum in Bunker Hill, Indiana, on 21 April 2005.

3
F-14A BuNo 162698 of VF-14, USS *Enterprise* (CVN-65), October 2001

Issued new to VF-33 in September 1986, this aircraft saw combat in *Desert Storm* as the unit's CAG jet in early 1991. With the 'Starfighters'' disbandment on 1 October 1993, the jet was transferred to VF-32. The latter unit transitioned to the F-14B in 1996, and BuNo 162698 was passed on to VF-14. Seeing combat both in Operation *Allied Force* in 1999 and in OSW and OEF in 2001, the Tomcat served with the unit as its CAG jet for five years until sent to AMARC on 1 February 2002.

4
F-14A BuNo 161279 of VF-14, USS *Enterprise* (CVN-65), October 2001

Delivered new to VF-1 in August 1981, this aircraft later served with VF-191, VF-21 and VF-24, before joining VX-9's Det Point Mugu in late 1994. BuNo 161279 returned to the fleet with VF-14 in early 1999, and experienced combat with the unit in Operation *Allied Force*. More action followed in OSW and OEF two years later, after which the jet was transferred to VF-101 when VF-14 became VFA-14 upon its re-equipment with the F/A-18E. The aircraft was reduced to components as part of SARDIP at NAS Oceana on 29 December 2003.

5
F-14D BuNo 164600 of VF-31, USS *Abraham Lincoln* (CVN-72), October 2002

The fifth from last Tomcat built, this aircraft was delivered new to VF-124 in March 1992. With this unit's disbandment in September 1994, BuNo 164600 was passed on to VF-101 Det Miramar. In early 1997 the Tomcat was issued to VF-31, and during its seven years of service with the squadron, the jet was marked up either as 'Tomcatter 100' or '101'. A veteran of three deployments with VF-31, and having flown numerous TARPS and combat missions during OEF and OIF in 2002-03, BuNo 164600 was stricken on 16 June 2003 and sent to SARDIP.

6
F-14D BuNo 159618 of VF-31, USS *Abraham Lincoln* (CVN-72), October 2002

Originally built as an F-14A and delivered new to VF-124 in October 1975, this aircraft was the 17th of 18 A-models remanufactured as F-14Ds in 1990-91. Following a second spell with VF-124, and then VF-101, the jet was assigned to VF-31 in 1995. Having patrolled Afghan skies in August-September 2002, BuNo 159618 dropped two LGBs in OSW and 35 LGBs/JDAM (as well as expending 193 20 mm cannon rounds in a rare strafing run) in OIF as part of the marathon ten-month CVN-72/CVW-14 war cruise. Retired by VF-31 in June 2003, the Tomcat was sent to SARDIP later that month.

7
F-14A BuNo 161274 of VF-41, USS *Enterprise* (CVN-65), October 2001

The 400th Tomcat delivered to the Navy, this aircraft was initially issued to VF-1 in May 1981. Subsequently serving with VF-154, VF-213, VF-24 and VF-211, it joined VF-41 in late 2000 and replaced BuNo 161607 as the unit's CAG jet. Midway through the 2001 cruise, VF-41's CO discovered that his maintenance master chief had named the 11 Tomcats in the unit after his old girlfriends. Cdr Gawne quickly agreed to having these nicknames applied to the radomes of the aircraft, with 'Fast Eagle 100' being christened *Anna*. Dropping 29 bombs in OEF, BuNo 161274 was passed on to VF-101 in late 2001 when the 'Black Aces' converted to the F/A-18F. Seeing out its final months of fleet service with VF-211, the aircraft was flown to AMARC in October 2004.

8
F-14A BuNo 158612 of VF-41, USS *Enterprise* (CVN-65), October 2001

See page 41 for this jet's airframe/OEF history.

9
F-14B BuNo 161432 of VF-102, USS *Theodore Roosevelt* (CVN-71), February 2002

Delivered new to VF-143 in October 1982, this jet subsequently became the 24th F-14A upgraded into a B-model six years later. Issued to VF-74, it saw combat with CVW-17, flying from the deck of USS *Saratoga* (CV-60), during *Desert Storm*. Sent to VX-9 following the 'Bedevilers'' disbandment in April 1994, BuNo 161432 joined VF-102 in 1996. Transferred to VF-101 three years later, the F-14 returned to the 'Diamondbacks' as its CAG jet in early 2001. Handed back to VF-101 when F/A-18Fs were issued to VFA-102 in 2002, the aircraft was retired in March 2004 and sent to NAS Jacksonville for SARDIP.

10
F-14B BuNo 163225 of VF-102, USS *Theodore Roosevelt* (CVN-71), March 2002
See page 45 for this jet's airframe/OEF history.

11
F-14B BuNo 162920 of VF-102, USS *Theodore Roosevelt* (CVN-71), February 2002
Delivered new to VF-103 in August 1988, this aircraft saw combat with the unit (assigned to CVW-17) in *Desert Storm*. Transferred to VF-102 in 1996, the Tomcat served with the 'Diamondbacks' until sent to VF-101 in April 2002 following the unit's switch to F/A-18Fs. The jet was sent to AMARC and placed in war reserve in April 2005.

12
F-14B BuNo 162918 of VF-103, USS *George Washington* (CVN-73), August 2002
See page 91 for this jet's airframe/OEF history.

13
F-14B BuNo 162910 of VF-103, USS *George Washington* (CVN-73), August 2002
The first new-build F-14B delivered to the Navy, this aircraft was taken on charge by NATC Patuxent River in November 1987. Eventually issued to the fleet in 1994, the fighter was supplied to VF-102 when it transitioned from F-14As to B-model jets in June of that year. Subsequently transferred to VF-103 in early 1999, the aircraft made two deployments with the unit in 2000 and 2002 and then joined VF-101 in 2003. Stricken in October 2004, BuNo 162910 presently serves as a gate guard at NAS Key West, Florida.

14
F-14B BuNo 161435 of VF-103, USS *George Washington* (CVN-73), August 2002
Delivered new to VF-142 in November 1982, this jet was the 26th A-model upgraded into an F-14B. Reissued to VF-74, it saw action in *Desert Storm*. Subsequently flown by VF-101, NATC and VF-102, BuNo 161435 joined VF-103 in 1998 and remained with the unit until sent to AMARC in January 2005.

15
F-14B BuNo 163220 of VF-143, USS *John F Kennedy* (CV-67), May 2002
Assigned to VF-143 straight from the Grumman

plant in March 1989, this aircraft was transferred to VF-102 in 1994. It returned to VF-143 in 2001 following a spell in storage. The jet was sent to AMARC in March 2005 and placed in war reserve.

16
F-14B BuNo 161438 of VF-143, USS *John F Kennedy* (CV-67), May 2002
Also assigned to VF-143 fresh from the Calverton plant, but in January 1983, this F-14A was duly passed on to VF-142 and then VF-101, before returning to Grumman to be rebuilt as an F-14B. Reassigned to VF-101, it joined VF-102 in 1998 and VF-143 two years later. The jet was sent to AMARC in April 2005 and placed in war reserve.

17
F-14A BuNo 159428 of VF-211, USS *John C Stennis* (CVN-74), March 2002
See page 79 for this jet's airframe/OEF history.

18
F-14A BuNo 161612 of VF-211, USS *John C Stennis* (CVN-74), April 2002
Delivered new to VF-124 in October 1983, this aircraft later transferred to VF-154. Also experiencing fleet service with VF-1 and VF-213, it returned to VF-154 in the early 1990s and was based in Japan with the unit until sent to VF-101 in 1997. The fighter joined VF-211 in 2001 and was retired to AMARC in September 2004.

19
F-14A BuNo 161603 of VF-211, USS *Enterprise* (CVN-65), November 2003
Delivered new to VF-124 in July 1983, this aircraft later served with VF-21, VF-2, VF-24 and VF-213. Placed in storage in the late 1990s, BuNo 161603 joined VF-14 in early 2001 and saw combat in OSW and OEF. It was passed on to VF-211 in early 2002 when VF-14 converted onto the F/A-18E, and the jet remained with the latter unit until flown to AMARC in October 2004.

20
F-14D BuNo 164348 of VF-213, USS *Carl Vinson* (CVN-70), December 2001
One of the last Tomcats built, this aircraft was delivered to VF-124 in early 1992. Passed on to VF-31 in June of that year, it served with this unit until transferred to VF-213 when the latter re-equipped with F-14Ds in late 1997. Seeing plenty of combat in OEF (the jet featured a 48-LGB bomb tally beneath its cockpit), BuNo 164348 was left at home by the unit for its 2003 OIF deployment, but the jet did return to VF-213 ranks for the squadron's last war cruise with the F-14 in 2005-06. The aircraft was eventually sent to AMARC in March 2006 and placed in war reserve.

21
F-14D BuNo 164603 of VF-213, USS *Carl Vinson* (CVN-70), December 2001
See page 28 for this jet's airframe/OEF history.

INDEX

References to illustrations are shown in **bold**. Plates are shown with page and caption locators in brackets.